The Cape of Good Cooks

The Cape of Good Cooks

Sally Simson

DOUBLE
STOREY
a juta company

Photo Credits The majority of the photographs in this book were taken by Ilse Andrag, to whom the publishers and author are deeply indebted. The sources of the other photographs and the pages on which they appear are as follows: Annandale 53 (bottom); Dalla Cia 8, 15 (right); Decameron 85; Djakarta 61; La Masseria 70, 71; Martin Meinert 32–3; Meerlust iv, 3 (2nd from left), 6, 7, 9 (except bottom right), 10, 11 (except bottom right), 16, 17; Middelvlei 100, 101, 102 (top right and bottom left and right), 103; Muratie 76, 79; Nathan-Maister 40, 41, 42, 47 (top); Sally Simson 14 (bottom), 102 (top left); Sarah-Anne Raynham 21 (middle top), 104; Thelema 20, 21 (top right and bottom), 23; Villiera 95; Warwick 1, 24–5, 26, 27, 28, 29, 31

This edition, completely rewritten and redesigned, published in 2004 by Double Storey Books, a division of Juta & Co. Ltd, Mercury Crescent, Wetton, Cape Town, South Africa

First published 1994 by William Waterman

ISBN 1-919930-33-7

Photographic editor: Ilse Andrag
Page design and layout: Sarah-Anne Raynham
Cover design: Abdul Amien
Reproduction: Virtual Colour, Cape Town

Printed by Clyson Printers, Maitland, Cape Town

Contents

Foreword

I have known Sally Simson for more than 50 years, but since this is roughly the age to which she now admits, I must not pursue this matter in case there are any mathematicians among her readers. Sally's brother Nic and myself were great friends from the days of pre-primary at Western Province Preparatory School, and we were both rather scared of Nic's older sister Sally, who took it upon herself to try to control our youthful enthusiasm for mischief, such as turning the garden hose on passing motorists in Tennant Road, Kenilworth, from the bottom of the Simsons' garden.

When we left prep school, I saw neither Nic nor Sally for many years until, about 20 years ago, she arrived at my farm with one of my neighbours for an evening cocktail and, of course, the pieces clicked into place and we have now become very great friends.

Stellenbosch became infinitely richer the day Sally moved here to take up a position with what was then Distillers Corporation. Her wonderful sense of humour won her many friends in the Stellenbosch farming community. I doubt whether there is a single farmer in Stellenbosch who would not open his home and, of course, wine bottles, when Sally arrives to visit, to talk about another chapter of her book.

Sally's writing abilities are legendary, as illustrated by the many books she has written. However, her cooking abilities are also legendary. Many a story can be told by friends who have had a Sunday lunch at Château Sally, when she appears, immaculately dressed, telling how she has spent the entire morning in the kitchen. The story is ruined by the catering service van parked in her driveway. On one occasion, the caterers delivered soup in a pressure cooker, and while sipping large quantities of sauvignon blanc in the courtyard, there was a tremendous bang. The lid had flown off the pressure cooker and the bulk of the soup was on the ceiling. Needless to say, a wonderful soupless party was enjoyed by all.

Fortunately, this is not a cookbook, but rather a collection of stories about the farms and farmers of Stellenbosch, with a few recipes supplied by each farm. I suggest you pick a few and try them.

I wish Sally the very best of luck with her future writing and I hope all her readers enjoy this book as much as I have.

Stan Ratcliffe
Warwick Wine Estate

Introduction

This tip of Africa, with weather instead of climate, with vineyards that climb mountains, with oceans and pungent fynbos, is so very beautiful. Alas, man, the only one of God's creatures to have studiously achieved immorality, is drowning this uniquely lovely piece of the world under a suburban tide of development.

We therefore have to relish what we have all the more: skies so blue you can almost touch them; shouts of autumn colour; sunsets which stain mountains pink; green, green grass where egrets stalk, white as snow, and flocks of guinea fowl joggle, like feathered footballs. And, of course, those tight bunches of precious grapes that produce wines to gild any meal, and rescue quite a few!

When the first ships en route from Europe and the East called at this southern tip of Africa in the 16th and 17th centuries, they found a paradise – rich oceans, remarkable mountains, abundant water and apparently virgin countryside as far as the eye could see. The local inhabitants they met, the Khoikhoi herders, traded their cattle and sheep with the sailors, in exchange for pieces of iron and copper.

But there was not much in the way of fresh vegetables. So the Dutch East India Company, in need of a refuelling stop, sent Jan van Riebeeck to the Cape in 1652 to settle it and to raise food with which to fill the pantries of passing ships.

Pretty soon there were vegetable gardens, orchards and farms, and cattle, sheep and pigs were breeding gratifyingly. The settlers discovered the local fish – particularly relishing snoek, rock lobster, oysters and mussels.

Many of the first settlers had spent time in Indonesia and Malaysia and they brought with them slaves from these eastern countries. This collection of palates, unused to bland European food, craved and subsequently imported spices to give local cooking a jolt.

When the Huguenots arrived, in 1688, they added a certain refinement to the hearty, feisty dishes the Dutch and Malays were producing, and a number of 'Cape' dishes evolved. These were hugely enjoyed by the locals and passing visitors who called in at what was no longer 'The Cape of Storms' but 'The Cape of Good Hope'.

The food that was prepared at that time gave birth to a truly indigenous cuisine. Unremarkable meat, given a liberal dash of various eastern spices, became 'bredie'. Not particularly exciting mince was given a spoon of jam, a handful of raisins and almonds, a few dried apricots and a custard topping and was transformed into 'bobotie'. Chutneys ranged from gently sweet to gaspingly hot. No one just boiled or fried fish. They pickled it, infusing its relative blandness with mouth-warming spices.

The Cape's unique flavours are tasted at numerous tables, but there has also been much input from the rest of the world.

I am hugely privileged to have friends in these winelands who, apart from being passionate about wine, are enthusiastic about and innovative with food. They have been very generous in providing this book with some of their personal recipes.

Meerlust

A Gift of Abundant Friendship

Hannes Myburgh represents the eighth generation of his family on Meerlust, one of the oldest and most illustrious estates of the Cape. Meerlust has belonged to the Myburgh family for almost two and a half centuries (since 1756).

The farm was originally granted to Henning Hüsing, an illiterate German mercenary who supplied the Dutch East India Company with meat. Eventually, he became South Africa's first millionaire, owning scattered grazing rights as far as Saldanha Bay.

Meerlust is a beautiful place. Its old walls glow gently, its lovely curling gables are etched against dark thatch. Flocks of guinea fowl patrol the vineyards and startlingly white ducks paddle on the dams.

The homestead is one of the very few of the time built of stone. This was quarried directly in front of the site and, finally, the holes were filled in and fenced off with squat, white pillars to make two flower gardens safe from marauding sheep. The front portion of the house was added to Hüsing's original by the first Myburgh on Meerlust and bears the date 1776. The curve of the gable clearly echoes the dome of the mountain behind it and, from inside the hall, Table Mountain is precisely framed in the open top half of the front door.

Meerlust has a long history of hospitality. In the late 18th century, Lady Anne Barnard described a meal at Meerlust: 'They reveal their dinners piano, piano, with what we should recognise as ordinary fare. Stewed cow-heel, which is a favourite dish, tripe, macaroni water-saucy and fish, but increase the size and number of their dishes every course, ending at the last with enormous joints.'

Thankfully, all that excess had diminished dramatically by the time I ate Sunday lunch at the table of Hannes's father, Nico. It was still a 'joint' meal – chicken roasted off the bones, potatoes in crunchy armour plating, baby peas in wafts of mint. This pungent herb also garnished Nico's pre-lunch G&Ts, to which he added a dash of bitters. In winter, in front of the roaring fire, Nico replaces the G&Ts with his own sherry blend – three-quarters medium cream topped with dry. It warms you up quicker than an electric blanket.

Today, there are dignified lunches and dinners at Meerlust, sometimes in the elegant dining room, more often in the kitchen with its garage-sized fireplace and acre of glossy table on which reclines a small, stuffed crocodile. The espresso machine wheezes cheerfully in the corner and Bettie Brown presides over the stove.

I love lunch with Hannes on the back stoep, especially in autumn when the vines that curtain it turn scarlet and the garden beyond is a wild tangle of late roses and pungent lavender. It is always a lot of fun.

And if Bettie serves her chicken curry, you can kiss the afternoon goodbye, because winemaker Giorgio's Italian palate is unused to spicy heat and, in self-defence, he keeps opening more cooling chardonnay.

Giorgio Dalla Cia, winemaker on Meerlust for years, is a master of cabernet and merlot, but I believe chardonnay is his great love. He revels in the challenge of releasing the complication of flavours inherent in this apparently simple grape.

In the dim, thatched cellar with its 300-year-old, metre-thick walls, serious and informed assessment of wine generally takes place. But sometimes flights of imagination and poetry intrude. Like the day someone dug deep in his cellar and brought along some really ancient French bottles and Giorgio produced some of Meerlust's long-nurtured gems.

It began with earnest talk of 'apples' and 'grass' and 'hints of mint' – or 'vanilla'. Then a little nuttiness intruded. John Platter inhaled 'fynbos' from the old chablis which made someone else sneeze convulsively. They decanted an elderly LaTache through a tea-strainer and Giorgio, taking a long pull, shouted 'Truffles!', a huge accolade in Italy.

Someone, delicately dragging a restrained sip of an antique Château Latour over his palate, yelled 'Bündner Fleisch!', which is a Swiss version of biltong, I gather. Thankfully I have never tasted dried buck in my wine. Someone else, commenting enthusiastically on one of Giorgio's chardonnays muttered, 'What a body! What long legs!'

Yet another taster touched on the constant changes in ageing wine and Hannes murmured, 'Just like us, dying as we speak.' We were tasting one of only two bottles left of Meerlust's '86 Merlot. With extreme courage I suggested we have the other one for lunch. And, by God, we did!

Then there is Hannes's annual Offal Competition, a contest to dress up that unmentionable contribution to life: tripe. On an autumn day we gathered on the lawns, glorying in sunlight newly released from rain-sodden skies, glasses full, laughter bouncing. In the kitchen, in stern contrast, taut characters were putting the finishing touches to their own particular version of that unspeakable dish concocted of unmentionable organs.

When they could escape for a moment, the competitors, treacherous smiles in place, mingled on the lawn. 'You look great, Sally!' said one. 'Love your hair,' said another. I preened, until a more alert friend scoffed, 'You aren't falling for that, are you?' and I realised the immoral hussy was merely touting for my vote.

Eventually, the kitchen crowded, cooks campaigning blatantly, guests heckling and barracking, the dishes were presented and tasted, then voted on by secret ballot.

What a con! I mean, tripe is tripe – plus or minus an onion or two. Not with this bunch, though. There was Gilly Stoltzman, who stretched tradition so far she imported curry spices from Durban, so we had a hot number. There was Elzbieta Rosenwerth, who clothes the glamorous and, being Polish, stretched 'farm kitchen' credibility even further by dousing her concoction in vodka. And, to encourage seconds – and votes – served a tot of it with every helping.

And then there was Bettie Brown, loving boss of Meerlust's kitchen. Ample, apron-swathed Bettie served TRIPE, proper, glutinous, falling-apart guts smothered in onions, a traditional treatment with which she wins the competition more often than not. She also, bless her, hides a bit of chicken in the oven so I can sneak something decent to eat.

A few years ago there was a well-researched restoration of the late-16th-century barn built by Henning Hüsing. When completed, the barn became home to a huge, imported, two-column still. Today, it is not brandy that purls through the old barn, but grappa, that ancient essence of Italy, which is probably older than written history.

No self-respecting Italian home or restaurant is without grappa and espresso, a combination which sparks words, ideas and laughter at the end of every meal.

Meerlust Grappa has, from the beginning, been assiduously tended by Giorgio's son, young George. With a stunning stroke of imagination he found a chocolate-maker to enclose sips of the liqueur in rich, dark chocolate. Then he found someone to create grappa ice-creams – a chocolate version, a vanilla one and, of course, a cappuccino.

Salute, Meerlust!

8

(Left) Hannes Myburgh represents
the eighth generation of
his family on Meerlust
(Bottom right) Hannes's nephew
George Landman is actively
involved in Meerlust

9

Young George's Meerlust Grappa Cocktails

Pinot-Chardonnay Grappa Cocktails

These cocktails are unique, elegant, sophisticated and were created specifically for Meerlust Grappa.

They make one serving and should be served in a Martini glass as they are all short cocktails.

DEATH IN VENICE

2 tots Meerlust Grappa
½ tot Campari
1 tot gin
ice
shake and strain

GRAPPARI

1½ tots Meerlust Grappa
½ tot Campari
ice
stir and serve

CORKSCREW

1 tot Meerlust Grappa
120 ml lemonade
½ tot blue Curaçao
ice
stir and serve

GRAPPA MARTINI

1 tot Meerlust Grappa
½ tot dry Vermouth
ice
stir and strain

VENUS FLY TRAP

1 tot Meerlust Grappa
120 ml fresh orange juice
1 tsp grenadine
crushed ice
stir and serve

GIORGIO'S COCKTAIL

1 tot Meerlust Grappa
1 tot Nachtmusik
stir and serve

STONE WOMAN

1 tot Meerlust Grappa
½ tot Cointreau
½ tot lemon juice
ice
stir and serve

1695

1 tot Meerlust Grappa
1 tot Kahlua
cola to top up
ice
stir and serve

BLUE MOON

1 tot Meerlust Grappa
1 tot Drambuie
1 tot blue Curaçao
lemonade to top up
ice, stir and serve

COCKTAIL CORRETTO

1 tot Meerlust Grappa
120 ml (chilled) espresso coffee
3 tsp sugar
ice
stir and serve

10

Cabernet-Merlot Grappa Cocktails

SENSATION

1 tot Meerlust Grappa
1 tot sweet Vermouth
1 tot dry Vermouth
ice
stir and serve

WINDSWEPT

1 tot Meerlust Grappa
½ tot crème de menthe
ice
shake well and strain

ECSTASY

1 tot Meerlust Grappa
½ tot D.O.M. Bénédictine
1 tot Grand Marnier
ice
stir and serve

AUDACITY

1 tot Meerlust Grappa
1 tot dry Vermouth
1 tot Grand Marnier
ice
stir and serve

BLUE GRAPPA

1 tot Meerlust Grappa
2 dashes blue Curaçao
2 dashes Angostura
ice
shake and strain

SCRUPLE

1 tot Meerlust Grappa
1 tot Calvados
1 tot lemon juice
ice
shake and strain

RAIN IN SPAIN

1 tot Meerlust Grappa
1 tot sweet Vermouth
ice
shake and strain

MAIDEN'S BLUSH

1 tot Meerlust Grappa
½ tot anise
1 tsp grenadine
ice
stir and serve

GIULIETTA'S

1 tot Meerlust Grappa
½ tot dry Vermouth
½ tot Cointreau
ice
stir and serve

SLAVE TO LOVE

1 tot Meerlust Grappa
½ tot Cointreau
½ tot Scotch whisky
ice
stir and serve

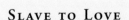

The Spirit of Italy

I went to Italy some years ago. It was the most amazing, heart-stopping experience, and a birthday present from my closest friends.

Hannes Myburgh had given a birthday dinner in my honour. It was great, and I was touched. But then he nudged a sort of pewter duck across the table towards me. 'There!' he said. 'Your present from us.' Well I looked at it, slightly taken aback. A duck? 'Go on,' said Hannes, 'open it!' Inside was a scrap of paper, telling me to pack a bag. This group of lovely people was sending me to Italy with the Dalla Cias. I'll never get over that present.

We arrived in Venice. Quietly, Giorgio and Simonetta guided me into the Palazzo. As we entered, sun streamed from behind clouds, lighting every arch and curve. Thousands of doves swirled and settled. If I hadn't had friends to hang on to, I think I would have collapsed, stunned.

We explored every inch of Venice, then we went on a long country weekend into the hills of Tuscany.

It was glorious. We stayed in a dear cottage looking over olive groves and vineyards, and a garden full of flowers. Simonetta was in a mood for deluxe cooking. We went for a long walk that evening. As we passed the only other house around I stopped to greet a cat that crossed the road. Out of the house bounced an elderly woman squealing 'Il gatto! Il gatto!', or something like that. It appeared she was apologising for her moggy's forward-

ness. Giorgio soothed her, and explained we were on holiday from South Africa. What did he do in Africa? she wanted to know. Made wine, explained Giorgio. That did it. Her husband made wine too – so we were forcibly urged through the house, down into an ancient, bottle-laden cellar and glasses were poured, far too gener-ously for tasting. Eventually our hostess laid the table in the cellar and produced bowls of steaming food while our host unplugged fresh bottles.

On this glorious holiday there were reverent moments, seeing Michelangelo's *David* and the spirals of an ancient church. There were spicy moments, such as inspecting an ancient olive oil plant and, for the first time in my life, tasting the oil fresh off the press. It was totally different from the usually quite gentle bottled oil. It

Sally Simson in Italy

'George, please pass me the oil'

was so fresh, so peppery, it made me gasp with delight. We drank wines in historic cellars, we ate, we laughed and explored. My taste buds have never been so alive and I was in a perpetual state of wonder.

Back home I have respectfully followed Giorgio on his early morning pursuit of the retiring *Boletus edulis* (cep) in the fresh pine forests. These mushrooms, designed by gnomes to shelter under, are hidden by cups of fallen pine needles. We stalk them in silence, because Giorgio is convinced they can hear you approaching.

His disgust, one day, when encountering other people on the hunt for his mushrooms in his secret forest was alarming. Leaving his forest (I dare not name it) after a rewarding hunt, we met a car on the same mission. Seeing our laden baskets, they grinned with delight and asked directions to the rich grounds.

I stood with mouth open, listening to Giorgio as he unhesitatingly mapped the route. He directed them to drive so far, then leave their car, climb the hills facing them and descend into the valley on the other side across miles of steep gorse and rough rock. They took off with alacrity and Giorgio turned to me, saying, 'They won't be back in a hurry!'

I am constantly amazed by Simonetta's old-fashioned attitude. According to her, the man is the boss, there are no decisions without the man, there are no engagements without the man. Home is sacred and the kitchen and the table its focal points. Yet beneath this apparent docility is a woman of huge patience and strength. I sincerely believe that there are times when, having been instructed by Giorgio on a certain theme, she apparently, docilely, and with no one realising it, does it in her own indomitable way.

Cooking is her passion and her pedestal. This doesn't mean Giorgio doesn't sometimes try to interfere in the kitchen – but he doesn't get far.

Simonetta teaches cooking around the generous table in front of a huge fireplace. She teaches groups of friends, people who know each other and share her enthusiasm.

Nipping from the table to the adjacent kitchen she produces and explains her own, authentic Italian dishes. The scholars listen in awe, sipping delicious Meerlust wine. They concentrate, they take notes and then they relish every mouthful. I went to a session once. As the meal drew to a close, the man next to me murmured, 'When this is over I am going to have withdrawal symptoms!'

15

Simonetta at Home

Risotto Zafferano

Serves 6

INGREDIENTS:

1 onion, chopped
2 tsp olive oil
1 tbsp butter
400 g arborio rice
3 litre good stock
½ tsp saffron
100 g Parmesan cheese

METHOD:

1. Sauté the onion in oil and butter, add rice, stir well until all coated and toasted.
2. Start adding the stock, one ladle at a time, and let the rice absorb it all before adding more.
3. Add saffron to taste, and cook for 18 minutes until al dente.
4. Top with Parmesan and serve.

Osso Buco

Serves 6

INGREDIENTS:

1 onion, chopped roughly
1 carrot, chopped roughly
1 celery stalk, chopped roughly
2 tbsp oil
6 osso buco (veal shanks) 3 cm thick
2 tbsp flour
1 glass white wine
400 g chopped tomatoes
salt and pepper to taste
some chopped parsley and lemon peel mixed together for the gremolata garnish

METHOD:

1. Fry the onion, carrot and celery in the oil.
2. Lightly flour the veal shanks and add to the vegetables. Seal the meat on both sides.
3. Add the wine and let the mixture steam for a few minutes.
4. Add the tomatoes, season to taste and add some water, to cover the mixture halfway.
5. Let it simmer for 2 hours, until the meat is tender.
6. Before serving, remove the meat from the pot, add the gremolata and let it simmer for a couple of minutes.
7. Pour the sauce over the osso buco and serve.

16

Pomodori Gratinati

Serves 6

Ingredients:

6 nice ripe tomatoes, halved
olive oil
oregano
bread crumbs
salt and pepper to taste

Method:

1. Preheat oven to 180ºC.
2. Place the tomatoes in an ovenproof dish sprinkled with some olive oil, add salt and pepper to taste and a touch of oregano, then throw the bread crumbs on top of each tomato and finish up with some olive oil.
3. Bake for 25–30 minutes until soft.

Thelema

Hard Work in Heaven

Something like 20 years ago, Gyles and Barbara Webb discovered a dilapidated farm covered in neglected orchards, dotted with crumbling buildings. And they fell in love with it. It took time, but they replaced the orchards with vineyards, restored the house, built cottages for staff and, of course, a winery.

So what grabbed them about this originally tatty place? It is, simply, one of the most beautiful farms in the Cape. It crawls up the steep slopes of the Simonsberg and looks out over a jumble of mountains with changing colours and depths of shadows, with sharp, rocky peaks and shoulders of fragrant fynbos. When the sun sets in summer the mountains are veiled in rose and gold. In winter they glisten with snow.

Now, Thelema is a mature and nurtured estate with beautiful gardens and vineyards that, just about every year, get Gyles the best vineyard award.

The cellar they first built has had to be expanded hugely and today the Thelema wines are regarded, locally and internationally, as among the very finest of the Cape.

I got to know Barbara and Gyles years ago when I rented their cottage for a while. I have never lived with views like that. It broke my heart to leave there. Apart from the human warmth and friendship, there was a clutch of tail-thumping dogs and a flock of peacocks, one of whom, Henry, became almost a house guest. He pecked at closed glass doors demanding entry and socialised with me and my visiting friends, round the table or on the stoep in the evening, when the sight of those lustrous mountains frequently throttled conversation – despite the open bottles at hand.

Barbara is gentle and very strong and, of necessity, extremely patient. She is one of those nuts who runs – not jogs, runs – at around sunrise every morning. She manages the business of Thelema, handling huge and complicated sales for the local and international markets.

She also gives strong-fisted, skilled massages. Or she did. I haven't enquired since the one and only time she 'did' me. I was laid face down on a table, with a convenient slit through which I could breathe and amiable dogs could lick my nose while Barbara hammered away at my back. It was great until I eventually clambered off the bed and Barbs complimented me. 'It is a pleasure to massage you, Sally,' she said. 'You have no muscle tone at all.'

Ed McLean

She is not the only insulting Webb. I took an international wine luminary to Thelema. Someone was sent to find Gyles while I fixed up the VIP with a glass of something and started what I, a bit despairingly, hoped would be an erudite vinous conversation. We heard Gyles before we saw him. 'Didn't you read the notice on the gate?' he asked. 'It says no riff-raff allowed!' But it wasn't remotely funny when, at some huge, very formal tasting, Gyles took the stand to talk about his wine currently in the tasters' glasses. He ended up by expressing belief in its ageing potential, saying, 'It could, happily, become a VERY old wine.' Pause. 'Not', he continued, 'as old as Sally, of course!'

Thelema has great parties. To the annual carol service everyone brings their own picnic suppers, wine and blankets, and sprawls over the lawn. The music is loud and everyone joins in singing songs about Baby Jesus and Santa Claus. On one carol evening, in the midst of rolling Hallelujahs, Barbara's wonderful mother – Ed – whispered that she was bored with all this holy music. She disappeared inside and next moment the air was filled with rock 'n' roll and Ed was be-bopping energetically.

Then there was the time when my son Charles came back from Cyprus for the holiday and the Webbs invited us to the family Christmas lunch on the stoep, overlooking lawns and trees and mountain peaks. We ended up dancing on the lawn, and I seem to remember it was to Vivaldi.

I love Thelema. Ed presides over the tasting cellar. She will pour you a customary tasting tot of some wine and when you murmur something appreciative and presumably learned, she says, 'You like it? Good,' and fills your glass, which you then take onto the little stoep with a dog or two in tow to feast on the mountains and wait for Henry the peacock to screech 'Hello!'

Gyles Webb

Austrian Coffee Cake

Serves about 8

INGREDIENTS:

6 oz butter
6 oz castor sugar
3 eggs
6 oz self-raising flour
pinch of salt
300 ml strong coffee
sugar
1 tot rum
250 ml whipping cream
1 tbsp castor sugar
1 tsp vanilla essence
toasted almonds for decoration

METHOD:

1. Cream butter and sugar.
2. Beat in eggs and fold in the flour and salt with a metal spoon.
3. Place into a 20 cm diameter greased ring pan.
4. Bake at 190ºC for about 25 minutes.
5. Cool the cake.
6. Mix together the coffee, sugar and rum and pour over the cooled cake.
7. Soak the cake overnight in the coffee–rum mixture.
8. The next day, whip the cream, then add the sugar and vanilla essence. Mask the cake with the sweetened cream. Decorate with toasted almonds.

Barbara's Mediterranean Lamb Stew

Serves 8

INGREDIENTS:

2 kg lamb knuckle
4 large onions, cut into cubes
6 large cloves garlic, chopped
125 ml olive oil
125 ml lemon juice
6 sprigs rosemary
2 tbsp olive oil
350 ml white wine
2 beef stock cubes
salt and pepper
4 peppers (red, yellow and green), chopped
3 cloves garlic, chopped
2 tbsp olive oil
4 potatoes, cleaned and cut into small cubes
40 depitted olives

METHOD:

1. Preheat oven to 180ºC.
2. Marinate the meat and onions in the olive oil and lemon juice with sprigs of rosemary in between, for 2 hours.
3. Drain, reserving the marinade, and braise the meat in 2 tbsp olive oil. Add the marinade, plus the wine, stock cubes and seasoning.
4. Place the meat and liquid in a casserole. Put into the oven for half an hour.
5. Sauté the peppers and garlic in 2 tbsp olive oil.
6. Remove the casserole from the oven, add the pepper mixture and a few more sprigs of rosemary, and return to the oven, lowered to 160ºC, for 2–3 hours.
7. After an hour, check the liquid, and, if running low, add some more white wine or lemon juice. Add the potatoes and olives. Return to the oven for 1–2 hours.

Serve with rice and peas and a baguette or two to mop up the juices.

(Left) The tasting room
(Below left) Thelema's symbol,
the Phoenix rising from the ashes.
The Phoenix was Gyles's family crest
(Below) Gyles and Barbara

Warwick

Nothing Regimental about Warwick

At the close of the Boer War, Colonel Gordon of the Warwickshire regiment elected not to go home to England and bought himself a farm which he named Warwick, after the regiment. He planted fruit trees and raised cattle on it, so when Stan Ratcliffe bought the farm in 1964, there wasn't a vine on it.

But what a glorious place! It slopes gently then steeply to the top of Klapmutskop outside Stellenbosch. From the forested tip you can see Cape Point and the ocean, and to the north are the Simonsberg, Hottentots Holland and Helshoogte mountains, so close you want to reach out and touch their purple crevasses. In the evening, the sun, easing slowly below the sea in a gilded blaze, paints the mountains a translucent rose.

Stan planted some cabernet vines which did well, but being no winemaker and not even a gambler, he sold the grapes in bulk, until half a dozen years later, when he introduced his Canadian bride to her new home. Stan and Norma played around a bit in the elderly, primitive little cellar and then the passion toppled Norma. She was seriously addicted, so Stan, being a practical fellow, made a decent cellar for her and in 1985 they produced 1,500 cases of their very first Warwick wine. Today Warwick produces something like 20,000 cases and there still isn't enough to go round.

On Warwick's dining-room table there rules, courtesy of Norma, an antique loving cup. It takes the form of an elegant, silver figure in Elizabethan dress whose wide skirts, uptilted, create a generous beaker and who carries in her upraised hand another, tiny silver cup. Both were used to toast weddings and wagers. She now appears on Warwick's labels, and still does her regal round of the dinner table as Stan urges port on guests.

I must admit to interfering with the dignity of the Warwick Lady. One day, the Ratcliffes brought out a rosé wine, an unconventionally dry, cabernet-based refresher. It was a touch frivolous, perhaps, compared with the rest of their dignified stable. In an idle moment I drew a rather silly picture of the Loving Cup Lady in a jiving mood and – blow me down – they put it on their rosé label!

There is another strange label among the Warwick wines. Starting with the 2002

Warwick

ROSÉ

26

Norma   The Rats: Stan, Norma, Mike and Jenny   Mike

vintage, the sauvignon blanc picked from certain vineyards is named Professor Black. It commemorates the professor and a handful of scientists who, many years ago, had grown yellow cling peaches on that piece of land, crossing Kakamas and Keimoes varieties in an effort to produce an early ripening variety that would extend the normal picking season.

Warwick has expanded, of course. Son Mike is firmly in command of the business side and Norma now has a winemaker, but she still meticulously oversees the wine, deserting it only – in the off-season – to dash off and pedal a bike, hit a ball, run a mile, even to climb Mount Everest! Daughter Jenny is export manager of a major wine trading company and a Master of Wine. She is also one of the most innovative cooks in the winelands. Stan, calmly in the background, keeps an even keel, something he is used to, being an old yachtsman. He regularly takes his boat out, filled with friends, into Table Bay, even when the wind shrieks or rain pounds. Then he and his mates cruise the pub at the Yacht Club.

Entertaining at Warwick is simple for friends – a braai on the lawn next to the duck-freckled dam, with Stan, in shorts and chef's hat, in command, or a meal in the elegant dining room where Norma rules.

Sometimes there are wine lunches in the cellar, and here Jen, one-time owner of her own catering business, plays a big role – a deliciously creative one. When Norma first presented her Three Cape Ladies in 2000 – a cabernet, merlot, pinotage blend – Jenny's lunch ended with a trio of sorbets: a merlot and youngberry combination, a pinotage and cherry creation, and one of blackberries and frosted cabernet. Then there was the chardonnay lunch. First we were served smoked ham with a Dijon and chardonnay mousse, then fillet with a chardonnay-spiked béarnaise, and vegetables in a chardonnay vinaigrette.

I wonder in how many sophisticated gourmet corners of the world food is so meticulously geared to the wine instead of vice versa.

I love Warwick, its family, its wine of course – and its Bertie. Bertie is a ridgeback big enough to make Goliath cringe. I remember one tasting at Warwick, suddenly catching sight of Bertie starting up the ramp to the tasting-room. I turned to Michael Fridjhon and said: 'Chair! Get me a chair – quick!' Mike said comfortingly: 'Don't worry, Sal, he is a friendly dog.' I commandeered the nearest chair myself and sat, just in time to have

Bertie's front paws land firmly on my shoulders and his tongue enthusiastically wipe the make-up off my face.

When Stan comes round to my house for a drink, with Bertie, my cats, alerted by the sound of Stan's car, streak upstairs. I hunker down on the sofa in anticipation of Bertie's ruinous but dearly valued affection.

The Ratcliffes (also known as The Rats) and several other couples share a house up the West Coast, where about 300 hectares of the loveliest, wildest fynbos tumble down to stretches of sand against which the Atlantic hurls its foaming breakers. From the house perched above the beach, with binoculars, you can make out a couple of white dots on the horizon – the nearest houses.

One weekend Stan and Norma invited half a dozen friends to this house, each to bring some contribution to Sunday's picnic. Sunday turned out too windy to eat outside, so we laid it all out on the dining table and lit a fire in the grate.

Gourmets all, each contribution added lustre to the table, not least my artistically patterned little quail eggs. Stan himself saluted them as a great idea, until he swept his knife across the tip of one and drenched his shirtfront in raw egg. I thought the damned things were cooked when I bought them! I was summarily banned from the kitchen for the rest of my stay. So when the gang started throwing round the pots and pans, I took Bertie to the beach to stroll past seals dozing on the rocks and dare a toe into the icy brine. He has his uses.

Mike and Norma

Bertie, in unusually placid mode

Poached Pinotage Pears

Serves 4

INGREDIENTS:

250 ml black tea
150 mg white sugar
500 ml Warwick Old Bush Vine Pinotage
4 pears, peeled and cored (try to keep a few
  leaves on the stem)

METHOD:

1. Combine tea, sugar and 250 ml pinotage in a small, deep pot.
2. Add pears and bring to the boil. Simmer until pears are soft, but not overcooked. Test with a skewer.
3. Remove the pears from the pot, place in a bowl and allow to cool. Reserve the syrup.
4. Cover pears with the remaining pinotage (and possibly the rest of the bottle). This gives a wonderful deep colour.
5. Leave for 24 hours, adding a little of the syrup to ensure the pears remain covered.

TO SERVE:

1. Drain the pears, reserving the liquid.
2. Place each pear on a white plate (for maximum colour contrast).
3. Add a mixture of the wine and syrup according to the desired sweetness.
4. For a 'glossy' look, thicken the wine syrup slightly with 1–2 teaspoons cornflour and pour over the pears.

Pinotage Ice-Cream

Makes just over 1 litre

29

INGREDIENTS:

250 ml Warwick Old Bush Vine Pinotage
250 ml simple syrup – cook together 250 ml sugar and 250 ml water until sugar is dissolved. Cool. Can be made beforehand and refrigerated.
250 ml seeded pinotage grapes
250 ml cream
200 ml milk

METHOD:

1. Bring to the boil the pinotage, syrup and grapes. Simmer till fruit is soft and mixture is about half the original volume. Cool.
2. Add cream and milk and freeze in an ice-cream maker. (Without an ice-cream maker, place in a container in the freezer, and when the mixture starts to freeze, stir every 15–20 minutes until the ice-cream is set). If sweeter ice-cream is desired, more syrup may be added.

Mike's Special Winter Leg of Lamb (or a variation thereof...)

Serves about 8

INGREDIENTS:

5 spring onions, chopped

1 tbsp butter

2 tsp white wine vinegar

2 tbsp fresh white breadcrumbs

100 g blue Stilton cheese, crumbled

3 tbsp ground hazelnuts

1 cup raspberries or strawberries (fresh or frozen)

1.8 kg leg of lamb (de-boned after weighing)

salt and freshly ground black pepper

For the gravy:

4 tbsp Three Cape Ladies (a Warwick wine)

575 ml chicken stock

2 tsp cornflour

1 tsp Dijon mustard

140 g fresh or frozen strawberries

METHOD:

1. First make the stuffing. Cook the spring onions lightly in the butter to soften, add the vinegar and set aside.

2. Place the bread in a food processor and reduce to crumbs. Combine the crumbs with the cooked onions, then add the Stilton, hazelnuts, raspberries and seasoning.

3. Preheat the oven to 200ºC. Open the leg of lamb out and season well. Spoon in the stuffing, then tie up with string.

4. Place the lamb in a roasting pan and cook, allowing 15 minutes per 450 g, boned weight. When the lamb is cooked, transfer to a warm plate, cover and allow to rest.

5. Now make the gravy. Heat the remaining fat in the pan over the stove to concentrate the sediment.

6. Stir in the wine, add the chicken stock and simmer.

7. Measure the cornflour into a cup. Add the mustard and combine with 2 tsp cold water. Add to the roasting pan and stir to thicken.

8. Add the strawberries and season generously with freshly ground black pepper.

9. Carve the lamb and serve with buttered new potatoes and spring vegetables – and the gravy.

*Mike savouring a sip
from Warwick's 'Lady'*

The slave bell in the front garden

Stan's Vegetable Potjie

The ingredients given are per person.
Add greater quantities as needed.

INGREDIENTS:

1 onion

1 sweet potato

½ butternut squash

1 apple (preferably Granny Smith)

4 cloves garlic (more if desired)

1 tbsp butter

METHOD:

1. Peel all the ingredients and cut roughly into 2 cm chunks.
2. Place the onions in the bottom of a three-legged cast-iron cooking pot (otherwise known as the Mandela Microwave).
3. Mix together the sweet potato, butternut and apple chunks and add them to the pot.
4. Crush the garlic and add to the mix.
5. Place the butter on top of the veggies.
6. Place over a low-heat fire with the lid on and simmer gently until soft, stirring occasionally with a wooden spoon.

Serve hot at a braai and I can guarantee that the pot will be licked clean every time.

Martin Meinert

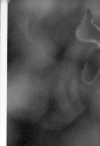

Where Synchronicity Reigns

Probably the most publicly memorable part of Martin Meinert's history was his stint as winemaker at Vergelegen. He was a vital part of the transition to their superstreamlined, numbingly expensive, sophisticated new gravity-fed cellar, buried at the top of a foothill. It was an enviable position, running this svelte number on one of the Cape's wealthiest and most historic estates, but – perhaps – not really Martin.

In 1987 he bought a farm of his own, Devon Crest Vineyards. It was only 16 hectares, but included one of the highest hills bordering one of the loveliest valleys on earth, Devon Valley, just outside Stellenbosch. There were a few vines on the land but, unfortunately, so blighted by leaf roll that Martin had to start all over again. It wasn't easy – in fact, Martin says, it was hell up in the top vineyards, which are practically perpendicular. Eventually he had some cabernet sauvignon, merlot and pinotage vines going, and in 1991 he built a small, unpretentious winery. Eventually he left Vergelegen and in '97 bottled his first Meinert wines.

When you drive up to the Meinert Winery there are two old, rose-draped cottages where Henk, the farm foreman, and Koos live with their families. You are greeted by a couple of huge dogs who, hearing the sound of Martin's vehicle approaching, go into a frenzy of enthusiastic wagging and yipping.

The cellar is simple, basic, quite small but very efficient, except for Martin's desk which overflows with a jumble of paper. He is in love with everything about wine and winemaking, except the business side. In these refreshingly unostentatious surroundings he makes his own wine, plus some wines for Devon Valley Hotel and for Ken Forrester of 96 Winery Road restaurant.

Martin's wines have an interesting label. His father owned a printing works in Namibia, and the company sports club used the crest of the German Master Guild of Printers as their emblem – a two-headed eagle with a printer's stick in one taloned claw and an ink roll in the other. Martin simplified the eagle, replaced the ink roll with a tasting vessel and put it on his label, on which, with typical sensitivity, he also uses the colours of Devon Valley: blue for sky, green for vine leaves, reddish-brown for the sandstone soils of the hillside.

What comes out of this winery is a fascinating mélange and says a great deal about Meinert's breadth of vinous knowledge and experience. The man didn't sit back on his

cum laude Viticulture and Oenology degree, nor on his employment in various prestigious local cellars. He has worked in France (at Château Lafite Rothschild, no less), Australia, New Zealand, Italy, Portugal, California … you name it. He is a man of broad experience, nuts about wine and food and jazz, sensitive to line and shape and colour, with a very philosophical bent and distaste for mediocrity, hence the name of his imminent new wine – Synchronicity. It is mainly cabernet sauvignon and merlot, with some cabernet franc, which is pretty routine, but then he has added an adventurous dash of pinotage. It's a wine made in the most demanding way, with no added yeast and no long maceration. Each variety is made and matured separately, then blended.

I love the brochure for this proud and hefty wine, suggesting dishes to eat with it. They include Prime-Rib in Balsamic Reduction, Guinea Fowl with Pearl Onions and Diced Bacon, and Springbok marinated in Spices and Red Wine.

Martin's feeling for line and shape is very evident in his house high up the hill with a view forever of mountains, vineyards, forests and ocean. It's heart-stopping. Each day, even when fog rolls in off the sea or the heavens open or the wind blows, Martin takes a few deliberate moments to absorb it. It is a house to dream of and, incidentally, has a kitchen which could not fail to inspire.

Henk, the foreman at the entrance to the Devon Crest winery

Roast Springbok Loin
(wrapped in Mango Atchar-coated Streaky Bacon)

'This recipe is very simple and quick to prepare and, most importantly, a perfect accompaniment to my full-bodied red wines. For a long time it was a big hit at our restaurant, 96 Winery Road, because of its wonderful flavour and because the meat remains beautifully juicy.

'This is a hearty winter dish which can be served with polenta or potato and roast vegetables.'

INGREDIENTS:

springbok loins, 1 per 2 people
streaky bacon, 2 strips per loin
mango atchar
olive oil
any Meinert red wine

METHOD:

1. Trim any sinew from the springbok loin.
2. Chop and mash the mango atchar to a paste.
3. On a chopping board, lay down lengths of string, then place the strips of streaky bacon on top of and in the same direction as the string. Now coat the bacon with a decent layer of the mango atchar paste and place the loin on top. No seasoning is required because the atchar provides enough.
4. Wrap the loin in the bacon and then tie the parcel firmly with the lengths of string.
5. Place about one tablespoon of olive oil in a pan and sear all sides of the loin briefly. In the meantime pre-heat the oven to 180ºC.
6. Place the loin in an oven dish and roast for approximately 15 minutes. It is best to watch carefully so that the meat does not overcook.
7. To make a sauce, de-glaze the juices in the oven dish with the red wine to the right consistency.

36

The cellar,
the Devon crest and
Noble Late Harvest wines

Devon Valley Hotel

Delicious Memories

Years ago, Devon Valley Hotel was so tatty no one went there except for an occasional sundowner, and that only because of the glorious view. You went inside only when in dire need of a refill.

Then came change. A sprucing-up and polishing that, while keeping its inherent country simplicity intact, turned it into a comfortable hotel. The garden now is a rich wilderness of beauty, the patio a tree-shaded expanse of sun-warmed brick overlooking a valley of vineyards and an arc of mountains that reaches the sea.

Here among the trees and bougainvillaeas, birds make happy sounds and a select club of cats loll supine on warm stone. (Actually, when I pitch up they stop lolling and approach in happy anticipation.)

David and Lee-Anne Nathan-Maister created this idyll. It was an extreme leap for David from his own computer business to hotelier. He exchanged his yuppie lifestyle for what he called bucolic bondage, his BMW sports for a muddy 4x4. Lee-Anne, on the other hand, who qualified as a chef under Southern Sun's Bill Stafford, resuscitated in herself a talent somewhat submerged by marriage and the computer culture. She supervised the food and dreamed up dishes which were awesome in their originality, taste and sheer number.

David comes from a highly musical family and has for a long time hosted a weekly show on Fine Music Radio. His mother is a music therapist for children with special needs, and his brother heads Drama at New York's Rochester University where musical theatre is a speciality. David claims no musical ability but has a passion for it, particularly its history and the vocal music of masters like Caruso, Gigli and divas like Maria Callas.

David's other passion, in his own words, is 'alcohol, in all its forms', which includes wine, naturally. The hotel's Sylvanvale range is made next door by Martin Meinert. It is an interesting range, consisting of two pinotages and two chenin blancs, each with one made from vine-dried grapes, which results in extreme intensity, plus a really interesting, dry cabernet rosé.

So, as you settle on the patio, letting the view enfold you, it would seem natural to select a Sylvanvale wine. But the decision is somewhat complicated by the wine list, which

carries 100 local wines, running from sherries through to muscadels and ports and including some rare vintages and auction wines. Then there are 20 or more imported wines from France, Italy, Spain, Hungary, Australia, etc., a whole page of cognacs, brandies, grappas and witblits, and three pages of single malts.

The whiskies are a major part of David's passion. A Scot on his mother's side, he is bewitched by the history and complete individuality of single malts. Where does their unique flavour come from? From the terroir? The water? The stills? Perhaps the personality of the distiller? There was a lot of conversation about this on the evening David gave a serious tasting of single malts. It was a table of earnest sniffers and sippers as the whiskies marched around. But then David Biggs started playing the bagpipes. Someone else got up and attempted a somewhat shaky Highland Fling and the cat took refuge on the stuffed moose head over the bar, known incidentally as Chocolate The Mousse.

Added to this alcoholic cornucopia of David's are two European devils of seduction. One is chartreuse, an ancient elixir still made according to instructions given to French monks in 1605, which included 130 medicinal and aromatic plants infused in wine. It is a drink with, supposedly, a legion of curative powers.

The other is absinthe. What a reputation! The Bohemian intelligentsia of the 19th century milked it for inspiration. Baudelaire and Verlaine scribbled furiously under its influence. So did Hemingway and Joyce. Degas honed his talents on it and it helped Van Gogh throw convention out of the window.

To overcome its bitterness, absinthe is drunk by 'louching' – pouring it slowly over a sugar cube poised over a glass. But nothing can diminish the hallucinogenic effects of the essence of wormwood it contains, an ingredient which can cause addiction and rowdy drunkenness. It was banned early in the 20th century, but today we have learned to drink it with cautious respect and it is back in the drinks cabinet.

Devon Valley Hotel is not all rural glory and alcohol – and this is where Lee-Anne comes in. From the start she inspired and ruled the kitchen with mind-blowing results. The menu – which changed often – emphasised local dishes like Butternut Soup with Malay spices, Guinea Fowl in Pinotage, Traditional Waterblommetjie Bredie, and Karoo

Lamb. But they were interspersed with flashes of soaring imagination, like Tomato and Gin Soup, Duck Breasts in Mango and Rum Sauce, Walnut-coated Crocodile Tail. And how about Fillet in a Malt Whisky and Olive Sauce, or Linefish in Pernod Butter? Naturally there was a Malt Whisky Parfait among the desserts and a sinful number called Devon Decadence, which is no exaggeration! This chocolate concoction has about ten million calories. I gorged on it one flowery summer afternoon, so greedily I was almost tempted to ignore the gentle plea for 'Cream, please?' from my favourite patio cat.

Devon Valley Hotel was sold suddenly but the memories remain, as does Lee-Anne's Devon Decadence. To my huge relief, the new owners have kept the essence and atmosphere of this garden of delight intact.

Franschhoek Smoked Salmon Trout on a Herb Crêpe

INGREDIENTS:

smoked fresh salmon trout, 3 slices per portion
mixed fancy salad leaves
cocktail tomatoes
dry pink peppercorns
fresh chervil or Italian parsley

Herb Crêpes:

(Makes about 15 crêpes)
12.5 ml freshly chopped mixed herbs
250 ml cake flour
pinch of salt
250 ml milk
1 egg
¼ tsp baking powder

Honey & Lemon Vinaigrette:

90 ml sunflower oil or olive oil
30 ml fresh lemon juice
30 ml warm honey
2 g salt and pepper
1 tsp pink peppercorns

Chive and Yoghurt Dressing:

200 ml yoghurt
70 ml chopped chives
2 g salt and pepper

METHOD:

1. First make the crêpes. Mix all the ingredients together until the mixture is very smooth.
2. Pour a thin covering of batter into a crêpe pan and cook.
3. Set the crêpes aside in a warm oven.
4. Blend all the vinaigrette ingredients in a blender.
5. Put all the dressing ingredients into a bowl and mix together.

TO ASSEMBLE DISH:

1. Place a crêpe on a plate.
2. Twist and arrange the salmon trout slices on it.
3. Arrange the salad leaves in the centre of the salmon.
4. Add the cocktail tomatoes.
5. Drizzle the vinaigrette onto the greens and the dressing onto the salmon.
6. Garnish with the peppercorns and chervil or parsley leaves.

43

Cape Seafood Bouillabaisse

Serves 8–10

INGREDIENTS:

1.8 kg mixed white fish fillets
1 kg white fish heads and bones
24–30 raw tiger prawns or langoustines (optional)
8 ripe plum tomatoes
1 tbsp Pernod
16 saffron strands

For the broth:

450 g onions
6 garlic cloves
1 head of fennel
450 g leeks
4 celery stalks
2 carrots
285 g potatoes (optional)
bunch flat-leaf parsley
125 ml olive oil
1 hen crab or shells of crab and lobsters
900 g tinned chopped tomatoes
2 sprigs of thyme
2 bay leaves
4 strips of dried orange peel
1 bottle of dry white wine, e.g. Sylvanvale
    Chenin Blanc or Graça
3 litres of boiling water

For the rouille:

10 saffron strands
± 1 tsp chilli paste
300 ml good mayonnaise

To serve:

1 thin baguette (French loaf) for croûtes
olive oil
115 g Gruyère cheese, grated (optional)

1. First make the rouille. Pour 2 tablespoons of boiling water over the saffron threads in a small bowl and leave to steep for 15 minutes. Add to the mayonnaise.

2. Season and stir in just enough chilli paste, a teaspoonful at a time, to achieve the heat intensity you find most pleasing.

3. Meanwhile, prepare the croûtes. Preheat the oven to 220ºC. Cut the baguette into 1cm slices.

4. Brush the slices on both sides with a little of the olive oil, arrange on a baking sheet and toast in the oven until golden brown. Check every few minutes, because they burn fast!

5. Now prepare the vegetables for the broth. Peel and chop the onion and garlic. Dice the fennel. Rinse and coarsely chop the leeks and celery. Peel and coarsely chop the carrots. Peel the potatoes and cut them into 2 cm dice. Destalk and chop the parsley.

44

6. Prepare the other ingredients. Remove the skin from the fish fillets and reserve. If using prawns or langoustine, shell and de-vein them and set the shells aside.

7. In a large heavy saucepan, fry the onion and garlic in the olive oil until translucent, taking care not to let them brown as this would ruin the flavour.

8. Add to the pot the fish heads, bones and any skins, as well as any prawn or langoustine shells plus crab and lobster shells.

9. Add all the vegetables, together with the canned tomatoes with their liquid, the thyme, parsley (reserving a good handful for garnish), bay leaves and orange peel.

10. Pour in the wine and the boiling water.

11. Bring to the boil.

12. Skim, lower the heat to a simmer and cook gently for 30 minutes.

13. Strain the broth through a sieve into a clean saucepan, pushing with a wooden spoon to extract all the juices.

14. Taste and season with salt and pepper.

15. Put to one side.

16. Blanch the tomatoes for 60 seconds in boiling water, refresh in cold water, then peel and dice. Add to the broth and bring to a simmer.

17. Add the saffron and Pernod.

The fish must be cooked just before serving – do not start this part until just before serving

18. Cut the fish fillets into large chunks and add to the broth.

19. After 3 minutes add the peeled, de-veined prawns or langoustines and crayfish. Poach for a further 2 minutes (5 minutes in total) when the fish flesh should be opaque and just cooked.

20. Transfer the cooked fish to a warmed serving dish. This makes it easier to apportion.

To assemble the bouillabaisse:

1. Place the fish in large soup bowls, ladle over the broth, scatter on some parsley, and serve.

2. Offer the croûtes, rouille and Gruyère at the table for people to help themselves by spooning some rouille on the bread, adding a spoonful of grated cheese on top, and then floating the slices in their broth.

45

Lee-Anne's Devon Decadence

INGREDIENTS:

450 g plain chocolate, broken in pieces
450 g butter, cut into cubes
200 g castor sugar
250 ml single cream
300 ml whipping cream
8 eggs

Chocolate glaze:

175 g plain chocolate chips
30 g butter
6 tbsp milk
2 tbsp golden syrup

METHOD:

1. Preheat oven to 180ºC.
2. Grease a 23 cm springform cake tin.
3. In a large, heavy saucepan over low heat, heat the chocolate, butter, sugar and single cream, stirring frequently, until the chocolate melts and the mixture is smooth.

4. In a large bowl, beat the eggs lightly with a wire whisk or fork. Slowly beat the warm chocolate mixture into the eggs until well blended.
5. Pour the mixture into the springform tin so that it spreads evenly.
6. Bake for about 45 minutes. Cool the cake completely.
7. When the cake is cool, carefully remove the side of the tin. Wrap the cake tightly with plastic wrap, still on its tin base, and refrigerate until it is well chilled (at least 6 hours).
8. Prepare the chocolate glaze. Heat the chocolate chips and butter, stirring frequently until the chocolate is melted and smooth. (If the pan is too thin it will transfer heat too fast and burn the chocolate.) Remove the pan from the heat and beat in the milk and golden syrup.

GLAZING AND DECORATING THE CAKE:

1. Line the cake plate with strips of greaseproof paper. Carefully place the well-chilled cake onto it.
2. With a palette knife, spread the warm glaze over the top and down the sides.
3. In a small bowl, whip the whipping cream until stiff peaks form.
4. Spoon the cream into piping bags. Round the top edge of the cake, pipe scrolls of whipped cream in a continuous circle.
5. Refrigerate the cake if not serving immediately.

46

Crème Anglaise

(For Devon Decadence and other desserts)

INGREDIENTS:

2 l milk
200 g sugar
20 ml vanilla essence
12 egg yolks
200 g sugar
100 g cornflour
400 ml milk

METHOD:

1. Boil milk, sugar and vanilla essence together. Make sure the milk does not burn on the bottom of the pan.
2. Mix egg yolks with remaining sugar.
3. Add cornflour and milk to egg and sugar, and mix until smooth. Pour into boiling milk and mix vigorously.
4. Bring to boil and cook until cornflour is cooked and has thickened.
5. Cover the sauce with greaseproof paper and refrigerate.
6. When required, correct the consistency with cream.
7. For cinnamon anglaise, add ground cinnamon to taste.

Leg of Lamb all'Abruzzese
Serves 6

INGREDIENTS:

700 g onions

3 large red & yellow peppers, about 700 g total weight – mixed works fine but green doesn't look nice

3 large red chillies

6 garlic cloves

salt and black pepper

2.3 kg leg of lamb or lamb shanks

50 ml olive oil

45 ml dried oregano

750 ml dry white wine

3 x 400 g cans whole plum tomatoes

METHOD:

1. Roughly chop the onions.
2. Cut the peppers into finger-length strips.
3. Finely chop the chillies.
4. Peel the garlic and leave whole.
5. Season the lamb well with salt and pepper.
6. Heat 15 ml oil in a large, deep, heatproof casserole or roasting tin and in it brown the lamb thoroughly all over. Set aside any burnt fat and discard it when cool.
7. Heat the remaining oil and fry the onions, peppers, chillies, garlic and oregano together over a medium heat, stirring occasionally, until beginning to brown, for about 5 minutes.
8. Add the wine and tomatoes, bring to the boil and bubble the mixture vigorously for 10 minutes.
9. Place the lamb on top of the vegetable mixture and season well.
10. Baste the lamb and cover with foil.
11. Cook at 170ºC, basting occasionally, for about four hours.
12. Uncover and cook until tender, about one hour.
13. Carve roughly into chunks. Serve with rice, noodles or polenta.

Whisky Parfait with Prunes and Earl Grey Syrup

Serves 12

INGREDIENTS:

300 g granulated sugar

300 ml water

1 tbsp Earl Grey tea leaves

32 prunes, soaked in cold water for 24 hours and stoned

1 tbsp lemon juice

75 ml whisky

5 egg yolks

300 ml double cream

75 g castor sugar, dissolved in 3 tbsp water

12 x 125 ml dariole moulds

METHOD:

Earl Grey syrup:

1. Dissolve the sugar in the water and boil gently in a large pan for about five minutes. Do not stir.
2. Add the tea leaves and allow to infuse for a further six minutes off the heat.
3. Pass the syrup through a sieve and add the prunes to the still hot liquid.
4. Season with the lemon juice and 25 ml of the whisky.
5. Place this in a tub, allow to cool, and store covered in fridge.

Preparing the parfait:

1. Whisk the egg yolks until very pale and increased in volume.
2. Whip the cream with the rest of the whisky until it starts to thicken.
3. Boil the castor sugar and water until it reaches the softball stage. To test, dip a cold teaspoon into the syrup, dip it into cold water to set and pinch the syrup between your finger and thumb. When it can be rolled into a soft ball, it's ready (116–118ºC). The syrup must still be white, not brown. (If your syrup is overcooked, your parfait will be too hard.)
4. With the mixer running at full speed, slowly pour the sugar onto the yolks.
5. Reduce speed by half and whisk for a further 5 minutes.
6. Fold the yolk and syrup mix and the whipped cream together and pour into the moulds. Freeze immediately.

To serve:

1. Heat four prunes per person in enough Earl Grey syrup to cover.
2. Remove the parfaits from the freezer, run the tip of a knife around the top of each one and rap on a hard surface to help release them.
3. Turn the parfaits out onto the centre of a plate.
4. Arrange four prunes around each and drizzle the syrup over it.

49

'n Boer maak 'n Plan

Hempies du Toit grew up on the farm Alto, where his father made wine and where he himself learned to make wine and play rugby. Eventually he became nationally known for both – for the wines of Alto, respected by every wine-lover, and for chasing balls for the Springboks.

Hempies is a huge man, barefoot even in mid-winter and devilishly mischievous. He is married to Naomi, serenely lovely and eternally patient, with a clutch of seriously talented children.

Hempies had to leave Alto when it was, rather summarily, sold. This was both traumatic and saddening, but the Du Toits refused to be overwhelmed and, with much courage, bought Annandale. This farm had been for many years a home for rescued horses – once abandoned, neglected or abused – where they grazed peacefully in lush meadows. Some who reached their end there are buried down Memory Lane along the riverbank. Those who survived their compassionate rescuer now live in Knysna with her descendants. Except for a few, Hempies still has them chomping idly away in the fields.

It is a wonderful farm, and the house has been restored by Naomi with minimal help. Under her calm, efficient care Annandale's garden blooms radiantly. It really is a masterpiece, with an old, old richness. There is a wild olive grove, and a riverbank where a bird-watcher once logged 96 species in one morning. Vineyards march up the hill slopes. On the peak of the highest hill, with mountains rearing at your back, you can look across to Table Mountain and its surrounding oceans. There is a little dam beside the horse paddock where a coastal coral tree grows. I'm sorry – I really still know it by its forbidden name, kaffirboom. But this tree is close to 200 years old! Hempies took me to see it once. Before its sensuous, gnarled limbs were in sight I saw a huge ibis in a nest above the placid water. Hissing at Hempies to hush (he was sloshing and slithering and muttering along the bank), I pointed upwards. Instead of reverent silence, the big oke raised a fist in salute and called 'Hey! Môre, Mamma!' The bird, without even changing position, cawed enthusiastically back to him.

Annandale's maturation cellar was built in 1700. It has thick, uneven walls, beams like tree trunks and blankets of ancient spiderwebs. Part of it has been tidied into an engaging and informal tasting-room filled with souvenirs and mementoes and is home to a couple of blindingly white doves who pace round the tasters' feet in utter calm, or roost peace-

52

fully on a shelf. Other doves nest and eat in dry seclusion in an old wine barrel in the branches of an oak outside the door and, when Hempies lets out his familiar holler, they descend on him from all directions. In winter, you can have a cup of soup with fresh bread in front of the fire to wind up your wine-tasting – with more wine, of course, or port, Hempie's deep passion.

Annandale is a supremely natural place and deeply endearing. I called in to see Hempies once. A clutch of enthusiastic dogs welcomed me to the sacred hub and there loomed Hempies, towering, arms outstretched and liberally clotted with clinging red grape skins, most of which he left affectionately on my shirt. He then advised me not to pat the most exuberant dog as he had been rolling in horseshit.

What workers these Du Toits are! With fierce determination, with absolute refusal to be daunted by severe economic restraints, they have nursed their Annandale from its strapped and primitive beginning to an efficiently productive farm with a cellar full of wines that are beginning to stun the wine-drinking world.

Last vintage I walked the vineyards with Hempies assessing the stages of ripeness of his various varieties. He picked one grape here, one grape there, tilted them to the sun to reveal the depth of colour in their juices, popped them in his mouth to taste, and spat the pips into his palm to check for any hint of lingering green in their beige maturity.

He does this every day until the grapes are at their peak and then rushes them to the cellar. Hempies has never made white wines and his reds seem to have inherited his robust character – a weighty, distinguished cabernet, a happy cabernet–shiraz blend and an elite port.

Naomi has been cooking for her family from breakfast through lunch to dinner for years. I must say she has done it with great forbearance and took the time to infuse imagination into her dishes, evident in the recipes that follow. And Hempies, like every other farmer, is a braai master. He actually invented the perfect portable braai – a wheelbarrow equipped with half a huge tin drum, which can be wheeled wherever desired – to the shade next to the river perhaps, or up into a vineyard where buzzards circle and Table Mountain turns russet at sunset. His relaxation time is well earned.

53

Pumpkin Fritters

Makes about 20 fritters the size of a golf ball

INGREDIENTS:

500 ml pumpkin, cooked and drained
2 cups cake flour
2 eggs
20 ml baking powder
25 ml sugar
2 ml salt
500 ml cooking oil

Sauce:

500 ml sugar
250 ml water
250 ml milk
15 ml cornflour
12.5 ml margarine

METHOD:

1. First make the sauce. Put all the ingredients except the cornflour into a saucepan and bring to the boil. Mix the cornflour with a little water and pour slowly into the boiling or cooking mixture.
2. Keep the syrupy sauce simmering while you cook the fritters.
3. Mix all the fritter ingredients together.
4. Pour the oil into a deep pan, heat it and deep-fry golf-ball-sized dollops of the mixture until done.
5. When done, throw the fritters into the simmering sauce.
6. Lift out immediately and keep warm in oven. Dish a little of the remaining sauce over the fritters and serve.

Bobotie

Serves 4

INGREDIENTS:

450 g best beef mince
2 medium onions, chopped finely
1 tsp butter
1 tsp turmeric
2 slices brown bread
2 tbsp raisins
1 tbsp tomato sauce
1 tbsp chutney
1 large apple, grated
1 tbsp curry powder
1½ tbsp vinegar
salt and pepper to taste

Topping:

2 beaten eggs
1 cup milk
2 bay leaves or lemon leaves

METHOD:

1. Brown the mince and onions together slowly in the butter.
2. Mix all the other ingredients together. If the mixture is dry, add a little water. It must be quite wet.
3. Mix this into the mince and onions.
4. Simmer for 10 minutes.
5. Put into a baking dish.
6. Beat the eggs into the milk.
7. Pour on top of the mince mixture, lay the bay or lemon leaves on top, and place the dish into another dish filled with warm water.
8. Bake at 180ºC, until the custard has set.

Vegetarian Lasagne

Serves 6

INGREDIENTS:

2 onions, finely chopped

1 tsp butter

3 packets washed spinach or Swiss chard, with any hard centre removed from leaves. If using chard, chop it up

2 rounds feta cheese (any flavour)

1 tin tomato-onion mix

250 g mushrooms, sliced

1 tsp butter

1 tsp powdered vegetable stock

1 box lasagne sheets

white sauce, about 1 litre (pouring consistency)

a little mozzarella cheese, grated

METHOD:

1. Soften onion in a little butter.
2. Add the spinach and cook until done.
3. Drain all the excess liquid.
4. Put the mixture into a food processor, crumble the feta rounds into it and blend until smooth or to your preferred texture.
5. Take a baking dish, and pour the tomato and onion mix into it.
6. Cook the mushrooms slowly in one teaspoon of butter with the vegetable stock powder until there is no liquid left. Layer the mushrooms over the tomato-onion mix.
7. Place a layer of lasagne sheets on top of the mushrooms. Just before layering the lasagne sheets, dip them quickly in water. This helps the sheets to soften when cooking in the oven.
8. Pour a layer of white sauce over the lasagne sheets.
9. Divide the spinach mixture into two, and lay one half on top of the white sauce layer.

10. Repeat the layering sequence, ending with white sauce as the last layer.
11. Sprinkle the grated mozzarella on top.
12. Bake in the oven at 180ºC, for half an hour. (Allow to stand for about half an hour before cutting.)

Djakarta

Antiques, Roses and Exotic Spices

I succumbed instantly, the first time I walked into Djakarta. It was so unexpected. Outside it was just a simple suburban house with nice trees, but nothing striking. Inside, however, it had been adapted as a restaurant with such taste – gleaming wood, snowy tablecloths, great bowls of fresh roses, cosseting winter fires. And then we drifted outside, and I was hooked. And that is where I eat whenever the temperature allows, which happily is about three-quarters of the year. There is a vine-covered stoep that surveys two big, reed-edged fish ponds and a green, grassy hill backed by blue sky. And around the ponds, trailing in all directions, is a rose garden – not neat and geometric, but enthusiastic, where the roses grow in apparent freedom, touching the world with their serene, enigmatic colours.

I could use 'enigmatic' to describe Indonesian food, but certainly not 'serene', with its exciting spices and mouth-tingling chillies.

Duncan was born in Batavia but then spent considerable time in The Netherlands, where he learned about the native Indonesian food from his Indonesian, cooking-polished grandmother and his food- and cooking-passionate father.

After years in the profitable but not very creative real estate trade, Duncan took a daring leap into the restaurant business and ended up just outside Stellenbosch on the M12, opening Djakarta. It is another world, loaded with oral thrills you have never encountered, some with mouth-frying chillies, which even Duncan admits are 'for looking at only'.

Irresistible peanuts and roasted coconut can be sprinkled on any dish, even on Sambal Goreng Telor – which are moreishly spicy eggs. My particular downfall is the Green Thai Chicken Curry with a wild medley of imported Oriental herbs and spices and coconut basmati rice.

There is the whole gamut of the Indonesian *rijsttafel*, which consists of at least nine different dishes, each an unimaginable experience for the novice. If you are really too chicken for these bold foreigners, you can settle for the old Cape standby – Fish of the Day.

Duncan Fransz

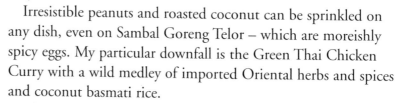

There is more to Djakarta than exotic food. The stretches of prolific roses are not just there to admire. They are sold by the bunch, fresh off the bush. And, hidden away, is a big, ramshackle sort of barn filled with incredible antiques, many from the East, with exotic, sensual swirls and twists. There are beds, tables, chairs, music stands, cupboards and plenty of more unusual items. Duncan restores them when needed, and sells them.

Yet another facet of Djakarta is the periodic wine-tastings in the charming, wine-packed little room off the dining area. Generally on the last Wednesday of the month, a local winemaker brings wines for diners to taste before they eat, and presumably gives advice as to which wine to drink with which dish – although I personally would leave that entirely to Duncan.

A view of strawberry fields from the stoep

Ayam Goreng Yogya
(Seasoned Chicken Dish)
Serves 8

INGREDIENTS:

3 onions, chopped
1 tbsp galangal (fresh, dried or ground)
1 tbsp ground coriander
1 tsp red bell pepper, chopped
2 tsp cumin seeds
4 candlenuts
¼ cup vegetable oil
3 lime leaves
2 tsp lemongrass stalk, finely chopped
1 tbsp dark brown sugar
1½ tbsp red chillies, finely chopped
1 kg chicken breast fillets, cut into 2.5 cm pieces
4 peteh beans (stinky beans)
4 cups coconut milk

METHOD:

1. First make the spice paste in a blender: mix the chopped onions, galangal, coriander, red pepper, cumin and candlenuts; then fry it in vegetable oil until the mixture foams.
2. Mix together the lime leaves, lemongrass, the sugar, and chillies.
3. Fry the chicken pieces at a high temperature until light brown.
4. Add the spice paste and lemongrass mix, as well as the peteh beans.
5. Add coconut milk and let simmer for 10–15 minutes.

Sajoer Lodeh
(Mixed Vegetables in Coconut Milk)
Serves 8

INGREDIENTS:

1 block tofu
½ cup vegetable oil
half a cabbage
5 big carrots
500 g green beans
1 lb tin bamboo shoots
one litre water or vegetable stock
1 tbsp galangal, sliced and lightly crushed
1 red pepper, sliced
4 chillies
6 peteh beans (stinky beans)
1 cup coconut milk

Spice paste:

2 onions, chopped
1 tbsp minced garlic
2 candlenuts
½ tsp shrimp paste
1 tbsp ground coriander
1 tbsp sugar

METHOD:

1. Deep-fry tofu in oil until light brown. When it is cool, cut into 2.5 cm pieces. Set aside.
2. Shred cabbage, slice carrots, cut green beans, slice bamboo shoots.
3. Boil water or vegetable stock.
4. Add lightly crushed galangal, sliced red pepper and chillies.
5. Mix together the ingredients for the spice paste. Add to the stock mixture, together with the vegetables and the cut tofu, peteh beans (stinky beans) and coconut milk.
6. Cook slowly until vegetables are almost cooked.

60

Babi Ketjap *(Pork in a Sweet Soya Sauce)*
Serves 8

INGREDIENTS:

1 kg pork shoulder

3 tbsp ground ginger

1 tbsp black pepper

1 cup vegetable oil

4 onions, chopped

2 tbsp crushed garlic

1 tbsp shredded fresh (or ground) ginger

5 tbsp stock made from pork bones, offcuts and vegetables (or vegetable stock)

8 tbsp thick Indonesian soya sauce

METHOD:

1. Cut pork into 2.5 cm squares. Marinate for 5 hours in the ginger, pepper and oil.

2. Fry the meat in the oil until light brown. Set aside.

3. Fry the onion, garlic and ginger until glassy, add the stock and meat and boil over slow heat until the meat is very tender.

4. Add soya sauce at the very end. Babi Ketjap tastes best the day after it is prepared.

Delheim

Snails, Olives and Earthworms

It must be 20 years ago that Vera and Spatz Sperling, two people of courage, energy and imagination, made a simple gesture to visitors and buyers at Delheim by offering a cheese platter under the trees, on the patio that looks across the winelands and distant flats to Table Mountain.

Spatz, a leader of the Cape wine world, has since turned Delheim into one of the eminent Cape estates, with a long and comprehensive list of wines involving a huge diversity of tastes and prices. Spatz and Vera have now, officially, taken a back seat and let their son, Victor, and daughter slowly take over. So they tell me.

Certainly the young Sperlings have a huge wine legacy to handle. The most up-to-date cellar is capable of handling something like a thousand tonnes of grapes and from these are produced an awesome number and variety of wines. I am not sure of the exact number but it must be around twenty wines, which range from noble classics to cheerful, everyday drinking, including the semi-sweets so many people enjoy rather furtively, a Cap Classique bubbly and 'Edelspatz', one of the Cape's most seductive Noble Late Harvests.

There have been big changes over the years. The modest cheese table has been transformed into a full-scale restaurant, small and cosy. But the great flagged patio outside, shaded by a gigantic jacaranda and cushioned with shrubs, is still the major attraction.

Ducks quack amiably or, at certain hours of the day, demandingly, on the patio. A couple of highly contrasting, scarlet-feathered chickens keep them company.

The restaurant is adaptable. You could have soup and an open sandwich there, or lamb shank or even a curry. You could finish your meal with their home-baked cheesecake with gooseberries and a drop (or so) of Edelspatz, a sinfully rich Noble Late Harvest from Riesling grapes.

Years ago Vera took up with the vineyard snails. She had hundreds and, after all the necessary steps, she simmered the

Cycle of life:
(Above) Delheim Vineyards
(Left) Spatz Sperling surveying the
damage caused by a forest fire

Spatz, his son Victor and daughter Norah

wretched molluscs in her broth with onion, herbs and parsley. I have never been able to eat a snail, but I know and respect lots of people who say they were sublime.

Nowadays Vera's attention is focused on olives. A few years ago the Sperlings planted 80 trees and a couple of years back began serious harvesting. Vera bottles them, uses them in the restaurant and sells them in the little farm shop.

The outdoor patio restaurant

Pumpkin Cubes in Spicy Liquid

This conserve is made at Delheim and served at its restaurant. It is also sold in its shop.

INGREDIENTS:

2.5 kg pumpkin, peeled and cubed
½ litre vinegar
½ litre water
1.5 kg sugar
1 cup vinegar
1 cup water
10 cloves
thin lemon and orange peel
juice of 2 oranges

METHOD:

1. Put the pumpkin cubes into a bowl with the first amount of vinegar and water. Cover, and leave in a cool place overnight.
2. The next day, combine the sugar, cup of vinegar, cup of water, cloves and peel, and bring to the boil.
3. Take the pumpkin cubes out of their first mixture, drain them and place into the boiling clove-and-peel liquid. Boil slowly until 'glassy'.
4. Take out the cubes with a slotted spoon, and pack them into a sterilised glass jar.
5. Add the orange juice to the leftover liquid and bring to the boil. Pour the liquid over the pumpkin cubes.
6. Seal and leave for at least three weeks.

Ripe Black Olives

(Original recipe from Ria Mars)

INGREDIENTS:

ripe olives
water to cover
salt for curing liquid
dark vinegar to cover
olive oil

For the brine:

4.5 l water
300 g salt
250 ml vinegar

METHOD:

1. Cut the olives on one side.
2. Place them in a bowl of fresh water so that they are covered, with a weight on them to keep them from floating.
3. Replace the water twice daily for 14 days.
4. Drain the olives, then cover them with salt water – 500 g salt per 5 litres of water – for one week.
5. Rinse off the salt water and place the olives in dark vinegar for 24 hours.
6. Take the olives out of the vinegar and allow them a few hours 'breathing' time.
7. Pack the olives in glass containers and add 10 ml olive oil to each.
8. Add a combination of herbs and spices, such as garlic, black peppercorns, rosemary, red pepper, oregano, thyme and bay leaves.
9. Now make the brine. Boil the water with the salt and add the vinegar.
10. Fill the bottles with the boiling brine. Enjoy after six weeks or longer in the bottle.

66

The conserve

An Italian Celebration

Miki Ciman has made cheese in several parts of the Cape. Then, some years ago, she and her husband, Lorenzo, took over an old, somewhat decrepit barn on a farm at the end of Blaauwklippen Road outside Stellenbosch. The barn looked over a tree-shrouded river straight up the multiple slopes of the Helderberg. It was glorious. All the barn needed was a good coat of paint. But Miki and Lorenzo had no time for that – they moved the cheese equipment in, did something about a kitchen, installed some tables and chairs, and called it La Masseria.

Doesn't sound like much of a restaurant, does it? But we had some of the best ever times there. The view was enrapturing, you were greeted like missed friends, the food was different, wine wasn't priced over the moon. And then – at some stage – the whole place suddenly soared in popularity because Lorenzo came out singing wonderful songs that everyone knew, in Italian of course, accompanied by Stanislav on his piano accordion. I've known people to leave their tables and start dancing.

It was great. However, there was a spate of developments on the farm, and Miki and Lorenzo had to go. Now they have a popular restaurant in the Kleine Eversdal manor house in Durbanville and at Ruitersvlei Estate, outside Paarl. They cater here and there for parties as well.

The cheese is now made in the La Masseria Cheesery at Delvera, where Miki's brother, Don, is in charge. There is an undecorated, basic tasting-room. Behind it is a proper factory set-up with icy rooms where the cheeses are made and slightly thawed ones where the cheeses are matured to a huge variety of different ages. There's Mascarpone, Provolone, Taleggio, Fior di Monte, Ricotta and – to be avoided at all costs – the decadent Duetto Dolce, in which preserved figs and walnuts have been scrambled up in creamy Mascarpone. Taste it once and you will be seriously addicted!

Incidentally, besides warming the world with his voice, Lorenzo also puts in time in the chilly cheese rooms, making his salamis with skill and precision. Now this is a touch of real Italian.

Farfalle al Salmone e Mascarpone

(Bow-tie Pasta with Smoked Salmon and Mascarpone)
Serves 6

INGREDIENTS:

1 tsp butter
200 g smoked salmon
500 g farfalle pasta
2 heaped tbsp mascarpone
1 heaped tbsp chopped parsley
freshly ground black pepper

METHOD:

1. Heat the butter in a small saucepan.
2. Tear the smoked salmon into small pieces and add to the butter.
3. Cook lightly so as not to let the salmon cook through. At the same time put a pot of salted water to boil.
4. Cook pasta as per instructions – drain well when pasta is al dente (with a bite).
5. Add the mascarpone to the salmon and heat through.
6. Put the drained pasta in a bowl and add the salmon sauce and toss well.
7. Sprinkle with ground black pepper and parsley and serve.

Quaglie alla Masseria

(Roast Quails La Masseria Style)
Serves 6

INGREDIENTS:

350 g ricotta
salt and freshly ground black pepper
6 slices coppa (Italian cured meat), chopped
a small bunch of sage
6 medium quails (deboned)
olive oil

METHOD:

1. Set the oven to 180ºC.
2. Prepare the stuffing by mixing the ricotta with a fork, add salt and ground pepper to taste, plus the chopped slices of coppa as well as half the sage leaves.
3. Stuff the birds with the ricotta mixture and put them in a roasting tray.
4. Dress with a little olive oil, salt and pepper, and the rest of the sage leaves.
5. Roast for about 25 minutes or until the birds are golden brown.
6. Serve on a bed of rocket or a mushroom risotto.

Muratie

Where the Past is Cherished

Muratie is a glorious place, of such simple, aged beauty and with such an intriguing background.

In 1699, when a Prussian émigré, Laurens Campher, was granted this land on the slopes of the Simonsberg by the governor of the Cape, Willem Adriaan van der Stel, it was virginal. Campher then married Ansela van de Caab, the daughter of a slave, and the two of them planted the first vines on what was later to be Muratie.

In 1763 another Prussian took over the farm. This was Martin Melck, who arrived at the Cape as a simple Dutch East India Company soldier, but became one of the Cape's first entrepreneurs. He made a fortune in building materials and stock farming, then became one of the Cape's leading wine farmers.

In fact, for 20 years he was the primary producer of wine and brandy at the Cape. Melck built a splendid mansion on what is now Elsenburg, the Agricultural Training College, the front door of which was later removed by Cecil John Rhodes and installed at Groote Schuur. Melck did a great deal for the community, including donating land and a building to the Lutheran Church in Cape Town. The church still stands, and the adjoining Martin Melck House is now The Gold of Africa Museum, both of them touching reminders of past elegance.

The next character to come to Muratie was Georg Paul Canitz, a German artist who arrived in Stellenbosch in 1910. He lived and worked in the village for some years. One day, when he was out riding, he happened upon the rather run-down but still incredibly beautiful farm. A close friend, Dr Perold, then viticulture professor at Stellenbosch University, encouraged Canitz to buy it, despite its dilapidated state. So Canitz did and christened it Muratie, from the Dutch word for 'ruin'.

Canitz and Perold made quite a combination. The one, a talented, eccentric Bohemian given to somewhat excessive partying; the other, a Karoo-born winemaker whom the South African government had sent to France and North Africa to study wine. When Perold returned to the Cape, richer by several languages and prodigious wine knowledge, he was appointed to the first Chair of Viticulture and Winemaking at Stellenbosch University. It is rumoured that he smuggled Barlinka winestock into the Cape disguised

Paul Canitz's painting, the Siren, watches over the tasting cellar

in a bundle of walking sticks! It is fact that he created pinotage, by crossing hermitage and pinot noir, which became the Cape's very own, individual grape variety and which has battled its way to international appreciation.

With Perold's guidance, Muratie was replanted, the first pinot noir vines in the country were established, the vines flourished and the wines sold well. Canitz, still painting, was exhibiting in London, Paris and Hamburg, and Muratie, gently restored to great beauty, became something of a social legend. Beside his studio, Canitz added a tiny 'drinking room', known as The Chapel, where hilarious, night-long parties of music and booze often took place. Departing guests covered the walls of The Chapel with appreciative graffiti and ladies hung scarves and empty perfume bottles from the chandelier, doubtless hoping to be invited again.

In 1988 Muratie once more belonged to a Melck. Ronnie Melck, directly descended from Martin, was a man with an abiding passion for wine, an incredibly acute palate, with a real joy for life and a shining sense of humour. Head of Stellenbosch Farmers' Winery, he brightened the whole wine industry. There was no chance of any wine event retreating into pompous dullness if Ronnie was anywhere in sight.

Now Muratie belongs to his family – his wife Annatjie and his two sons – one a lawyer, one a sometime doctor.

Not long ago, Rijk Melck, succumbing to a long-simmering yearning, abandoned his Stellenbosch medical practice for rustic Muratie where he is now general manager, coping with the vineyards, cellar, bottling lines, office, etc. Being a man of few conventions, Rijk is planning to open a small room on the farm so he can still consult for those patients who refuse to be dropped.

In today's world where medicine can be big business and one's doctor a barely recognisable member of some partnership, Rijk is a gift. One morning I had a paralysing pain in my back. Rijk came at once, gave me a jab in my butt and put me firmly to bed. He wanted to know what I had done the day before – not, he told me firmly, in my social life, just a step by step report, from bed to kettle to cat bowls to buttering toast and back to bed. I remembered – it was Tuesday, so I had taken the garbage out first before going back to bed with my tea and toast. 'Stay out of the garbage,' said Rijk. 'You're too old for all that crap!'

Muratie is an exceptionally lovely farm on the surging foothills of the Simonsberg. Vineyards tilt in every direction, assiduously scoured for insects by snowy ducks and a herd of grotesque turkeys. The house, built in 1830, is a gem, modestly hidden by trees and ebullient shrubs. The cellar is 200 years old. Canitz's studio is now a very comfortable bed and breakfast, from the patio of which you can watch the sun set behind Table Mountain. The tasting-room is thick-walled and yellow with age, adorned with comfortable furniture, some of Canitz's paintings plus a couple of wicked caricatures of Ronnie Melck, and shelves of Annatjie Melck's home-made preserves.

Annatjie, Ronnie's widow, lives in Muratie's main house and has built herself a booming – if eccentric – Stellenbosch business, Oom Samie se Winkel on Dorp Street, which has been around for decades. It is a restaurant in an old shop. Several rooms in the historic house are filled with an incredible clutter of old things – books, pictures, mugs and jugs, ancient tins, animal heads, frilly hats ... it is a mad and appealing collection.

But for me, it is the food on sale here that really intrigues. Annatjie, a really knowledgeable food-lover, has gathered a kitchen bouquet of delicacies: sweet chilli sauce, packets of buchu leaves, bottled garlic, home-made mustard, Khoisan sea salt with garlic and parsley or black pepper, tins of crocodile pâté with port, home-made jams with real chunks of fruit, sun-dried apricots in syrup, spices for bobotie and curry, and a corner of alcoholic exotica – Wild African Cream (a cream and liqueur combo that begs for ice-cream), mampoer, rooibos liqueur, etc. – plus a very unusual collection of vintage wines. There is also a wine-garden restaurant at the back.

This is such a food-oriented family, they even cook to order on the farm. Kim is Rijk's wife and, perhaps, the most lustrous talent. Herewith her most special recipe.

Snow right up to the back door

Springbok Venison Leg

Serves 8-10, with vegetable accompaniments

INGREDIENTS:

1 springbok leg

brown vinegar to fill container halfway up
    thickness of meat

1 tbsp vegetable oil

1 flat tbsp margarine

2 cups boiling water

1 medium onion, studded with cloves

4 pieces pork 'spek'

white pepper

coarse salt

5 rashers bacon

1 large cup apricot jam

gravy mix

METHOD:

1. Submerge the leg in brown vinegar for one day and one night. Remove the leg and discard the vinegar.

2. Preheat a large black iron pot with a lid. Combine the oil and margarine and add to the pot.

3. Place the springbok leg into the pot and, using your hands, roll the leg around just enough until it is seared all over.

4. Add boiling water, onion studded with cloves, pork 'spek', plenty of white pepper and coarse salt. Drape the leg with the bacon.

5. Put the lid on the pot and simmer gently until the meat is tender (it will take about 5 hours).

6. Discard the onion. Pour off one half of the liquid and reserve.

7. Liberally smear apricot jam over the leg and leave to rest for a few minutes while you mix up the gravy.

8. Carefully put the leg onto a serving platter with the 'spek' around it and add the gravy mixture to the rest of the liquid in the pot. The acidity of the gravy should be sweetened with apricot jam – never sugar!

9. When the gravy is the desired thickness and sweetness, your meal is complete!

This looks stunning on a big meat platter and is dead easy to do. I even managed to go shopping while the leg simmered alone at home.

It is best served with quince jelly, baby peas, caramelised carrots and thick cheesy white sauce over al dente cauliflower. The best part is that it keeps. Place the leg in two layers of tin foil, pour half the gravy over it, wrap it up and freeze for up to one month. Take it out the night before you're going to eat it and warm it through in an oven for at least ±1½ hours. It will be a huge treat and a surprise to take along with you on a weekend visit.

Rijk's Favourite Dish, to eat and cook!

INGREDIENTS:

1 kg Karoo leg of lamb
balsamic vinegar
coarse salt
white pepper

METHOD:

1. Wipe the lamb with a little balsamic vinegar. Season it heavily with coarse salt and white pepper.
2. Place in a roasting pan inside a cooking bag with a little water, just to get it going, Put it in an oven preheated to 180ºC and leave for 1 hour.
3. You can add a few sweet or ordinary potatoes and small onions, for vegetables with a great flavour.

Rijk and Kim

Decameron

Dali Fish in Pasta Heaven

When small, grey-mustachioed Mario, with his built-up foot, started Decameron, the general prediction was that he would see his whatsit and it wouldn't take long either. It is so long ago I have forgotten how many years, and it is still the business lunch joint in Stellenbosch and pop-in place for informal dinners.

Mario is as welcoming as the smell of hot bread. They automatically put me at a small table in an elevated position in front of the fish tanks. Wine-writer Dave Hughes (he is more than this, but how else do I describe him?) regularly has the other table there. He, because he likes watching the Salvador Dali fish; me, because I like the rather superior position from which I can watch who is coming and going.

I have always regarded taking doggy bags home from restaurants as being very undignified, in fact rather common. I was disabused of this notion by radio presenter Nigel Murphy. He was shovelling leftover fish into a plastic bag for his moggy, and, when I raised a disapproving eyebrow, he thrust the bag at me and said, 'Take it home to yours then, you'll see!' I did. Never mind the boiled hake, the chicken breasts, the best Pamper; this buttery, grilled kingklip slightly browned at the edges and sea-moist inside had them somersaulting in gastronomic ecstasy. Obviously I threw pride away and have since become an adept cat-bagger, even begging for other people's leftovers.

I did this once too often in Decameron and Mario scolded me soundly for 'Interfering widda clients!' Instead, he said, I could 'Bring da god-damma cats to lunch onna da house'. I swear I will one day.

Kingklip Maria

Serves 4

INGREDIENTS:

4 fresh kingklip steaks
250 ml water
sea salt
olive oil

Sauce:

50 g capers
4 garlic cloves
10 fillets of anchovy
250 g black olives, pitted
olive oil

METHOD:

1. First make the sauce. Put all the sauce ingredients except the oil into a blender, switch it on, and pour in the oil until a creamy consistency is gained. This sauce keeps for a long time in the fridge.
2. In a large pan, boil the kingklip in the water, covered, with sea salt and a drop of olive oil.
3. Cook until nearly ready, then remove the water, leaving ± 6–8 spoons of stock in the pan.
4. Add 2 tbsp of sauce and cook until the fish is ready.
5. If you need more colour and you are using a richer-tasting fish, add 1 spoon fresh tomato sauce, e.g. Napolitana sauce.

Linefish Decameron

Serves 2

This delicious dish is not fatty at all and is completely cholesterol-free. The simplicity of method complements the soft delicate texture of the fish. Cob/kabeljou is the most recommended linefish to prepare.

INGREDIENTS:

250 ml water
sea salt
2 fillets cob/kabeljou
1 ripe tomato, diced
fresh rosemary, sage and basil, chopped
Italian parsley, chopped
1 clove garlic, finely chopped
½ soupspoon lemon juice
1 tbsp olive oil

METHOD:

1. Boil the water in a large open pan.
2. Add sea salt and fish to the water (one or two pieces at a time).
3. Add the tomato, fresh rosemary, sage and basil, cover and bring to the boil.
4. Meanwhile, prepare the sauce by mixing together the garlic, lemon juice, olive oil and parsley.
5. When the fish is ready, put it in a dish, retaining some of the stock.
6. Serve the fish with the sauce spooned on top, and a little of the stock poured over it, together with fresh vegetables.

Penne Decameron

Serves 4

This recipe was inspired by the unique Stellenbosch region itself and in particular by the winter boletus mushrooms found growing wild in the forest encircling this beautiful valley. In order not to disappoint customers out of season, big brown mushrooms have been substituted, creating a unique flavour not unlike that of the wild boletus.

INGREDIENTS:

4 big brown mushrooms
butter
olive oil
brown sauce*
½ kg penne (durum wheat pasta)
pesto**
Parmesan, grated

METHOD:

1. Remove the brown filament from the mushrooms and slice.

2. Fry the mushrooms in a pan with butter and a little olive oil until the mushrooms relax and soften.

3. Add 4 soupspoons of brown sauce and cook for 5 minutes.

4. Meanwhile, boil the penne in abundant salted water for 9–10 minutes.

5. Strain the pasta and put in a large bowl with the sauce.

6. At the last moment add 2 soupspoons of pesto.

7. Add grated Parmesan to taste.

* Brown sauce: this takes about four hours to make but can be used in numerous other recipes. The basic sauce consists of off-cuts of meat, bones, and fresh vegetables, such as celery, carrots, onions, all cooked together in lots of red wine.

** Pesto: the recipe for this sauce, which consists of fresh basil, pine nuts, olive oil and garlic all pounded together, will be found in any good Italian cookbook.

84

Mario Ladu
in the Decameron kitchen; and
receiving the *Ciao Italia* Award
from Oscar Luigi Scalfero,
President of the Republic of Italy

85

Regretfully, only Once a Year!

Nicholas

St Vincent – chosen for the 'vin' in his name – was appointed patron saint of vineyards way back in the shadows of time. His feast day, on 22 January, is celebrated around the world with, first, prayers for the vintage soon to be harvested and, second, thanks for the vintage in the form of a right royal piss-up.

In Stellenbosch the wine folk gather on this day first at St Nicholas's Catholic Church, oak-sheltered in the middle of the dorp, which was, appropriately, a wine cellar in the 17th century.

There isn't much ceremony. The priests ask a blessing on the harvest, the congregation belts out a few favourite old hymns and then we all hightail off to lunch.

I remember my first St Vincent's Day, when Father Roger, in an Irish accent strong as whiskey, ended the swift proceedings by informing the congregation that everyone was now welcome up at 'La Pineta for a little something to eat and, hopefully, a great deal to drink!'

La Pineta is a simple, unpretentious but comfy place in a grove of squirrel-busy pine trees, with lawns where children and puppies gambol – and a view of strawberry fields and distant hills.

On St Vincent's Day, La Pineta's owner, Nicholas, once a priest himself, lets us unload as much wine as we like without charging a cent for corkage and feeds us generously and absurdly cheaply. Lunch can go on with laughter, stories and songs until the hills turn ruddy.

On one St Vincent's Day, Giorgio Dalla Cia, at the appropriate coffee-looming moment, rooted around in his cooler bag and produced a bottle of Meerlust Grappa, which was greeted with great enthusiasm by our table and several suddenly overly friendly nearby ones. David Nathan-Maister of Devon Valley eyed the bottle for half a second, took on a look of fierce concentration and started barking into his cellphone. The grappa tots were barely poured when a driver from Devon Valley scurried up, panting, and dumped a bottle of pale green chartreuse on our table. Now here was competition!

The Carthusian monks of Chartreuse have been distilling what was originally a medicinal elixir since the 17th century, a complicated concoction containing 130 different plants. The elixir is 71 per cent proof, and was presumed to be life-prolonging. It may not have kept one going longer, but it must have made the years available a blast. Only three Carthusian Brothers are allowed to distil the liquor today, each entrusted with only a third of the recipe.

St Vincent apart, La Pineta is a great, just-down-the-road joint, serving good, reasonably priced wine and imaginative cooking that doesn't make your wallet cower, and with a warmth of welcome that always makes me feel I have just come home.

St Vincent's Day dish
(La Pineta Chicken Hot as Hell)

Serves 6

INGREDIENTS:

6 deboned chicken breasts
6 slices sandwich ham
6 tbsp (60 g) grated Cheddar
12 slices bacon (streaky or back)

Hot as Hell Sauce:

1 medium onion, peeled and chopped
4 tbsp olive oil
6 red chillies, finely chopped
6 green chillies, finely chopped
4 garlic cloves, diced
2 tomatoes, skinned and chopped
½ tsp ground black pepper
1 tsp Worcester Sauce
1 tot brandy

METHOD:

1. Place chicken breasts between layers of plastic and beat until thin.
2. Place a slice of ham and 1 tbsp grated cheese on top of each chicken fillet and trim away the chicken 1 cm around the slice of ham.
3. Fold the fillets in half with the cheese in the middle, wrap 2 slices bacon around each fillet, and place in a greased oven dish.
4. Grill chicken breasts for 5–6 minutes on each side, under a hot grill.

FOR THE SAUCE:

1. Fry the chopped onion in olive oil until glassy.
2. Add the chillies and garlic and fry for a further 2 minutes.
3. Add the tomatoes, black pepper, Worcester sauce and brandy, and simmer together for about 10 minutes. If the sauce begins to dry out, add more olive oil.
4. Plate the breasts and cover each with the sauce.

90

La Pineta is famous
for its hospitality

Villiera

A Food- and Wine-Polished Family

Villiera is a happy place, a close-knit family affair. There is Jeff Grier in the cellar, sister Cathy in the office dispatching their wines around the world, and brother Simon in the vineyards. They are pretty special vineyards too, sprawling over gentle hills, bathing in sunshine, catching all the cooling breezes. And below the pebble pudding of their diverse soils lies a layer of clay, which means the vine roots are damply cosseted almost all year.

2003 was Jeff's twentieth year at Villiera, a farm originally consisting of 75 hectares bought by his father in 1983. It has since expanded to almost 300 hectares.

I think the mention of Villiera brings to most people's minds an instant picture of their festive sparkling wine, 'Tradition'. But the Griers produce a huge bouquet of wines which range from the simple, very reasonably priced but meticulously made to the more aristo-cratic classics. Among them are a traditional bush vine wine, a sauvignon blanc, several noble reds, more bubbly, a port and an irresistible Noble Late Harvest. There is a Villiera for every occasion, from a quick lunch in the kitchen to a wedding.

'Any favourites?' I once asked Cathy. 'No,' she said. 'They are like children, you can't have favourites.'

Kitchens play a large role in the Grier family. Their father was a chef and restaurant manager in France, then in Bermuda, then at the Edward Hotel in Durban. Simon reads cookbooks like other people read novels. Cathy studied food – and wine – in London, so is a gourmet chef and, incidentally, a Master of Wine. It is a family highly talented in two of life's happiest indulgences – food and wine.

Villiera has a tasting-room of almost rustic simplicity – brick floors, polished wood, some lovely paintings – which opens onto a huge shade-dappled courtyard to which, in summer, you can bring your own pic-nic basket (hopefully up to Grier culinary standards) with which to sip their pleasure-filled wines.

94

Simon Grier with Christie Frans and John Williams, Villiera management team

The Grier trio: Simon, Jeff and Cathy

Lamb in Spicy Beetroot Juice
Serves about 8

INGREDIENTS:

2 large beetroot, peeled and cut into eighths

1 litre water

6 cloves garlic, peeled

1 tbsp coriander seeds

2 tsp peppercorns

1½ tsp ground turmeric

1 tsp ground ginger

2 bay leaves

3 cardamom pods

90 g ghee (clarified butter – or you can just use plain butter)

5 medium onions, peeled and sliced

1 tbsp paprika

1 tbsp green chillies, chopped

1 kg deboned lamb, cut into cubes

250 ml yoghurt

1 tsp salt

juice of 1 lime (or ½ a lemon)

METHOD:

1. Place the beetroot and 2 cups of water in a saucepan. Bring to the boil. Reduce heat and simmer for 30 minutes.

2. Remove the beetroot and discard (or eat). Reduce the beetroot liquid by half.

3. Combine the remaining water, 5 cloves of garlic, coriander seeds, peppercorns, turmeric, ginger, bay leaves and cardamom seeds in a pan. Bring to the boil. Then reduce heat and simmer for 30 minutes.

4. Strain the spiced liquid into a bowl, and discard the spices.

5. Heat the ghee in a large frying pan. Add the onions and cook until golden. Crush the remaining clove of garlic, add the paprika and chillies and cook for 2 minutes. Remove the onions and chillies with a slotted spoon and set aside.

6. Add the lamb to the pan and brown on all sides. Add the spiced liquid and simmer, uncovered, for 30 minutes.

7. Stir in the fried onions, beetroot liquid, yoghurt and salt. Reduce the heat and simmer, uncovered, for a further 20 minutes.

8. Remove the lamb and onions with a slotted spoon and place on a serving dish. Reduce the remaining liquid to a rich glaze. Pour over the lamb.

9. Sprinkle with lime juice and serve.

95

Dry Fried Prawns on Mixed Salad with Roasted Rice

Serves 4

INGREDIENTS:

500 g raw, medium-sized prawns, shelled (you can substitute squid or a firm white fish)

4 tbsp oil

2 tsp paprika

5 cloves garlic, peeled and bruised with a rolling pin

2½ cm root ginger, peeled and bruised with a rolling pin

1 tbsp dry sherry

For the marinade:

½ tsp salt

1 tsp sugar

1½ tbsp thin soya sauce

2 tsp oil

pepper

For the salad:

300 g coriander

300 g mint

300 g rocket

2 tbsp rice, roasted in the oven or fried in a non-stick pan until brown

3 spring onions, chopped

1 red pepper, deseeded and chopped

handful of lemongrass

For the salad dressing:

3 tbsp Italian parsley, chopped

1 clove garlic, chopped

3 tbsp dill, chopped

3 tbsp olive oil

1 tbsp hazelnut oil

METHOD:

1. Slit the back of the prawns with a small sharp knife and remove the black vein (or you can buy the prawns where this has been done for you). Wash and pat dry.

2. Mix together the marinade ingredients and add the prawns. Leave in a cool place for 30 minutes.

3. Heat a wok (or heavy-based pan) until very hot. Add the oil. Add the paprika and fry for 1 minute. Add the garlic and ginger and fry for 1 minute, then remove and discard.

4. Add the prawns to the wok. Spread them out in a single layer and fry on one side for 1 minute. Turn over and fry the other side for 1 minute. Splash in the sherry along the rim of the wok.

5. Make the dressing. Place the herbs into a blender or food-processor bowl and switch on. Add the oil gradually until blended.

6. Mix all the salad ingredients and toss them in the dressing. Place the prawns on top and serve.

96

Villiera, being acutely concerned about the environment, has used no insecticides for at least 10 years. As a result the rodent population has increased. Trying to keep some measure of control, the Griers enthusiastically encourage owls to nest in comfort and pay their rent in rats.

(Left) The Patio of Peace

97

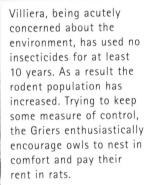

Middelvlei

Where Great Queen Sally Rules

Papegaaiberg (Parrot Mountain) dates back some 60 million years. It is a sudden, rocky outcrop on the edge of Stellenbosch where, early last century, Stone Age implements were unearthed.

Its name derives from an annual shooting competition among local farmers, which started back in 1685. The target was a wooden parrot perched on a pole at the tip of the outcrop. It was serious stuff, with cash prizes for the best shooters, and became an integral part of the birthday celebrations of Simon van der Stel, governor of the Cape, who gave his name to Stellenbosch.

Van der Stel was also the man who jolted local wine farmers when, revolted by the 'sourness' of our first wines, he started fining them for picking grapes that were not fully ripe.

Today, suburbs have encroached on the lower slopes of the mountain and you drive past their regimented little gardens to the gates of Middelvlei where, suddenly, the world widens into a huge bowl of undulating vineyards edged with distant mountain peaks.

Too many years ago to bear counting, I first visited Stiljan Momberg at his home on Middelvlei and fell in love with it. Often after that, Stiljan would escort me idly round the great green garden. First, it was to greet the shaggy, blond Himalayan goats with their curved horns and wild yellow eyes. They strike dramatically geometric poses on their long, spindly legs, wrestle horns with each other and thrust their faces towards you for a gentle scratch. Then came the spider monkeys which left their trees to skitter at our feet or squat on our shoulders or, occasionally, to dart down one's arm to nick a pawful of wine from a glass. We didn't walk the garden empty-handed!

Sometimes, a couple of monkeys would leap astride our accompanying dachshunds and, like jockeys, speed around the lawn while the dogs carried them, yapping in delight.

Stiljan Momberg in his own private fiefdom, 'Jan se Gat'.

Then Stiljan would steer me to the cellar under the house, his own private fiefdom, known with some irreverence as 'Jan se Gat'. Dim and cool, it was furnished with just a long table and some old chairs, but every inch of wall space was occupied by Jan's collection from some of the finest of this world's wineries.

100

Tinta with Tinta Barocca

There was one memorable lunch down there. Guests were greeted ceremoniously at the front door, guided past the empty dining room and down steep little steps into Jan se Gat – transformed for the day by a white tablecloth, silver cutlery and bowls of flowers. Each guest was presented with a menu and instructed, thus armed, to select whichever wine from the shelves they fancied with the fare.

Stiljan and his wife have now retired to the sea, leaving Middelvlei in the hands of son Ben, who tends the vineyards with genuine affection; son Tinnie, who makes the wine; assisted by younger brother Jan and their families; which brings in Ben's wife, Jeanneret, who manages the business and its wine sales, here and overseas, with awesome efficiency.

Stiljan still keeps his overstuffed chair in the boys' cluttered office and comes with advice, when needed – unless rugby is on or the fish are biting.

The animals and birds on Middelvlei all started out as rescued or orphaned and their numbers grow too fast to keep track of. There was a time when wine connoisseurs, sipping judiciously from their glasses, were occasionally confronted – to their initial consternation – by a cheerful young striped polecat, known in Afrikaans as a *stinkmuishond* because of the foul-smelling substance it sprays. Ben had found him, injured, in the woods, had a vet put him right and adopted him. The skunk lived in his pocket or on his shoulder for ages. Then, when Ben decided maturity meant the skunk needed a proper home of his own, he took the incredibly appealing creature back to the forest and spent hours digging with him until the skunk realised that this was really cool and decided to stay. Thereafter, Ben visited the skunk's den from time to time. He would scratch a bit around the hole and up came the skunk, to chatter and play with his lifetime mate.

All of Middelvlei's many animals are diligently and tenderly cared for, including the monster pigs. The family and a few wine-loving friends were lunching in the tasting-room one day. Suddenly, Ben left the table. When he returned he was toting a basket, which was squeaking ominously and covered by a cloth. Having got everyone's attention, some of it vaguely apprehensive, with a flourish he unveiled a litter of piglets – Vietnamese pot-bellied piglets actually. Four of them were there and then solemnly christened Platter, Biggs, Hughes and Sally. I wasn't sure whether to be greatly honoured or mildly offended,

David Hughes, Sally Simson, David Biggs and Erica Platter

but I can tell you that, years later, Sal is GREAT. Literally. She is the size of a short-legged cow, generally supine, very amiable and so fertile I can't count her progeny.

Middelvlei's official tasting-room, down in a gentle hollow by a lake, is a simpler version of Jeanneret and Ben's demurely lacy Victorian home across the meadow, one of only two Victorian houses on Cape wine estates.

The tasting-room is simple, welcoming and restful. It offers a cheerful fire in winter and, in summer, a table on the stoep overlooks vibrant green grass and shimmering water clotted with glossy geese. The goats are down there too, along with a couple of colossal, ancient tortoises, a family of buck, a rescued llama, all roaming contentedly, along with colourful chickens which look as if they are wearing purple and red knee breeches.

And the wines you can taste there! There's a gutsy cabernet sauvignon, a firm and full pinotage, a shiraz crammed with spicy fruit, and a chardonnay which, to me, has a wonderful crisp freshness. There is also an unusual pinotage–merlot blend which I once watched being tasted by some international expert. He took the tasting glass from Tinnie, did the routine eyes closed, sniffing bit – and gasped. He then glugged back his politely small tasting-tot and reached for the bottle.

102

Standing left: Ben and Jeanneret.
Seated from left: Kleinjan and Stiljan. On the right: Tinnie and his wife

Ben, Jan, Tinnie and Jan Junior Momberg

Momberg Manne's Smoked Snoek

METHOD:

1. Salt the vlekked open snoek lightly with coarse salt after purchasing and keep refrigerated.

2. Take a 200-litre drum cut open along the length and set it on a stand 45–60 cm high. Make a fire underneath the drum. When the drum is warm, take 5 handfuls of brandy cask shavings, which have been pre-soaked in water, and put them in the drum.

4. Remove the salt from the snoek and dry with a paper towel. Put it on a grid inside the drum.

5. Cover the drum with a piece of plywood, big enough to cover the opening completely. Smoke the snoek for between 10 and 20 minutes, depending on the size.

6. Serve with wholewheat bread, korrelkonfyt and sweet potatoes.

Aunt Mary's Sweet Potatoes
Serves 6

INGREDIENTS:

6–8 sweet potatoes, peeled
3 bananas
1 packet ginger biscuits, crumbed
6–8 tsp unsalted butter

METHOD:

1. Boil sweet potatoes until cooked, and cut into chunky pieces.

2. Layer the following in an ovenproof dish: sweet potatoes, bananas, crumbed ginger biscuits. Put pieces of the butter on top.

3. Bake in oven at 180ºC for 30–45 minutes.

103

Tinnie Momberg in his cellar

Jeanneret and Ben's 1905 Victorian home

David Biggs

David Biggs: Wine Nut, Cat Manicurist

There aren't too many serious moments with my friend Biggs. We go to a lot of wine-tastings together, more often than not in his home-made motor car, a convertible dart that causes audible gasps of appreciation and ruins my hair before we have covered two blocks.

We once deserted a couple that were just too ponderous to handle, played hookey and headed for my jacuzzi and a decadent g&t. Some while afterwards, Biggs was quite late for an event, busy with a radio broadcast. A lot of people had gathered on the lawns of the historic estate, and I was among them, when a stranger approached me, enquired whether I was, indeed, Sally Simson and then expressed great sympathy for the misfortune of my jacuzzi. She looked very puzzled when I asked what was the matter with it. Then a friend or two gave me words of commiseration as well. Eventually I discovered that Biggs had ended his broadcast listing places that anyone visiting the winelands should not miss. 'But there is one place to avoid at all costs,' he had wound up, apparently, 'and that is Sally Simson's jacuzzi.'

I remember a tasting at which the winemaker was waxing enthusiastic about screw tops replacing arm-wrestling corks. Finishing, he turned to David and asked if he would demonstrate the comparative ease of opening a screw-topped bottle. David gently twisted the cap. It gave a wild squeak and a snap as it opened. 'Crumbs!' said Biggs, 'sounds like Simson getting out of bed.' I get my own back, but not as often as I would like. I am obliged to keep in Dave's good books as he is the only person my cats will permit to clip their nails. When I decide the duvet can't take another threadbare patch and my best jersey is unravelling, I invite Biggs to lunch.

Dave has a daily column in the *Cape Argus* and has produced their weekly wine column for 23 years. He also writes for various magazines and is the author of six books on booze, among them *The Plonk Buyer's Guide*, which is in its tenth edition. Dave lives high on the mountain slopes overlooking the sea: a dizzyingly beautiful place to sit with a glass of wine and a couple of cats. Sometimes a whale churns the blue below, while across the glistening bay the mountains of the winelands rear their heads.

Dave Hughes

Dave Hughes: Clothes do Not the Expert Make

This is the undressed man. He refuses to be dragooned into conformity, never wears a tie – unless it is hidden under his beard just so as not to blatantly insult his host, and it has to be really frosty for him to get out of his shorts and thongs uniform.

There was one fearfully upper-crust reception and tasting at a certain cellar one Saturday morning. The management team were having words with their PR who had organised the do, because a few of the local farmers had pitched up in blue jeans. It was NOT the expected dress of the day, it was NOT good enough at all, even if it was not exactly Ascot. While the headman was explaining this to the embarrassed woman, the door clanged open to reveal another guest, Dave Hughes of international wine acclaim, with bare feet and shorts.

The thing about Dave is that he refuses to be smothered by convention. He has a crackling sense of humour and doesn't give a damn about the unimportant. Wine – and to some extent other liquor – has crowded his life and filled his brain for so many years that he is one of the most knowledgeable men in the world on his subject.

Dave is at every important wine event imaginable – one week he is in London for an international convention, the next he is jolling at the Calitzdorp Port Party. He has written more, tasted more, talked more than anyone I have ever met, on the subject of wine, and his enthusiasm never seems to wane. He is as in love with and fascinated by fermented grape juice today as when he first encountered it.

Dave remarried a couple of years ago and now lives in my favourite Devon Valley with Lorna – who is a viticulturist for some of the vineyards there. The two wine-mates make a perfect blend.

David Biggs's Apricot-stuffed Shoulder of Mutton

'I am fortunate to have a sheep-farming family, so I am given a shoulder of mutton from time to time. You will probably have to order yours from the local butcher. Get him to debone it for you. You will now have a large, flattish slab of meat.'

INGREDIENTS:

1 deboned shoulder of mutton
1 packet sun-dried apricots, chopped
3 or 4 cloves of garlic, finely chopped
a handful of dry breakfast oats
a bottle of hanepoot or jerepigo

METHOD:

1. Lay the mutton on the worktop and spread a generous helping of sun-dried apricots over it.
2. Sprinkle the garlic and the oats over it.
3. Now carefully roll the meat into a tight cylinder, and skewer it to keep its shape while you truss it neatly with cooking string.
4. Place the meat roll carefully in a roasting pan, skewer side down, then splash a liberal dollop of hanepoot or jerepigo over it.
5. Cover with cooking foil and roast at a low heat (130ºC) for 3 hours.
6. Serve with roasted sweet potatoes.

'A feast fit for a farmer.'

Dave Hughes's Butternut Soup

Serves 6

INGREDIENTS:

1–2 onions, chopped
1 large butternut, peeled and diced
1–2 potatoes, peeled and chopped
1 cup orange juice, freshly squeezed if possible
grated zest of 1 or 2 oranges
1 tbsp curry powder
2–3 cm fresh ginger, chopped
1.5–2 litre good chicken stock
salt and pepper to taste (I use white pepper as it doesn't make the soup look like it has floaters in it!)
1 large glass good sherry

METHOD:

1. Fry the onions in a large saucepan until glassy. Add everything else except the sherry.
2. Cook for at least 35 minutes, or until the butternut is tender.
3. Whizz up in a liquidiser and adjust the flavours.
4. Now drink the sherry.
5. Garnish with a swirl of cream and a splatter of chives.